ONE ANOTHER

A Guide for Strengthening God-Given Relationships

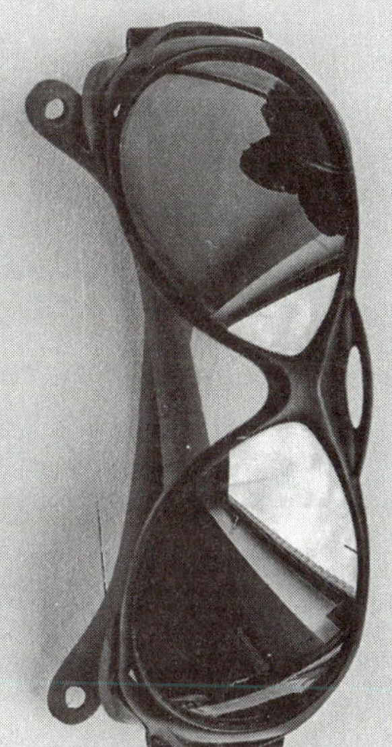

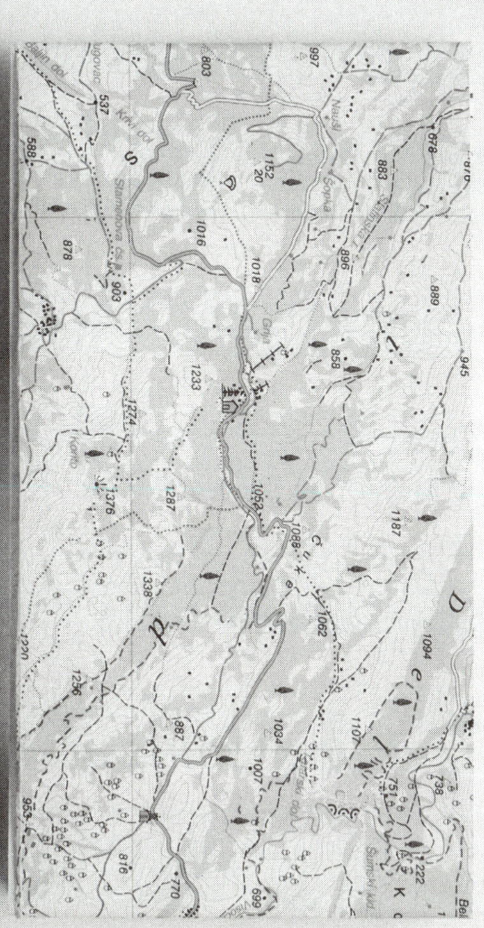

PAUL CHAPPELL

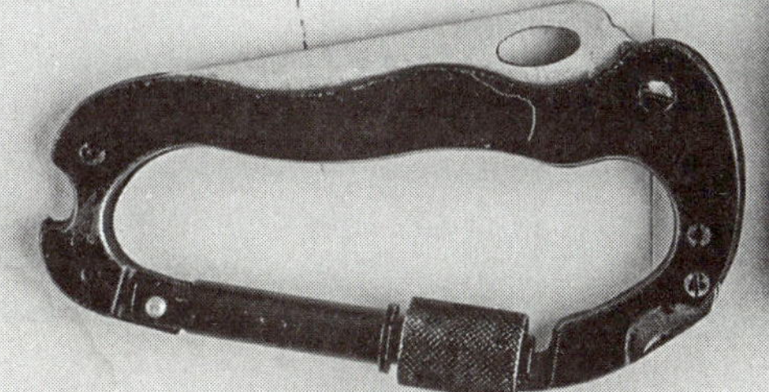

All Scripture quotations are taken from the King James Version.

First published in 2019 by Striving Together Publications, a ministry of Lancaster Baptist Church, Lancaster, CA 93535. Striving Together Publications is committed to providing tried, trusted, and proven books that will further equip local churches to carry out the Great Commission. Your comments and suggestions are valued.

Striving Together Publications
4020 E. Lancaster Blvd.
Lancaster, CA 93535
800.201.7748

Cover and layout design by Andrew Jones
Writing assistance by Anna Gregory, Denise Lee, Danielle Mordh

The author and publication team have put forth every effort to give proper credit to quotes and thoughts that are not original with the author. It is not our intent to claim originality with any quote or thought that could not readily be tied to an original source.

ISBN 978-1-59894-406-8

Printed in the United States of America

strivingtogether.com

CONTENTS

ABOUT THIS STUDY GUIDE

Here is a brief explanation of the features of this study guide:

OVERVIEW This section introduces the larger concept of the week's lesson. It is provided to acquaint you with the specific emphasis of each lesson, especially as it relates to previous lessons in the curriculum.

DISCUSSION QUESTIONS Each lesson is complemented by several questions to discuss with your group. These discussions can be rich times of learning from one another as you share experiences and insights.

LESSON NOTES Blank lines are provided for your notes as your group leader teaches through the lesson material. You may find it helpful to refer back to these outlines during your discussion time.

DEVOTIONS There are five devotions—each with a Scripture passage and devotional reading—for each week of this study. These complement the lesson material and are designed to be read the week after the group leader presents the corresponding lesson.

REFLECT Each devotion ends by asking what God spoke to you about as you read the Scripture and devotion. This question is meant to encourage you to take a few moments to meditate on what you've read and ask the Lord to speak into your life through it.

RESPOND This section gives you an opportunity to write down specific ways to apply the truths you are learning.

PRAY Each devotion concludes with a suggested prayer. You may find the written prayer provided helps you voice your heart to the Lord. Or you may choose to write or simply speak your own prayer as you communicate your heart to the Lord.

FOR AS WE HAVE
MANY MEMBERS
IN ONE BODY...
ALL MEMBERS
HAVE NOT THE
SAME OFFICE.

ROMANS 12:4

WEEK ONE

MEMBERS ONE OF ANOTHER

DAY 1: The Deception of Pride

DAY 2: More than a Feeling

DAY 3: The Pursuit of Peace

DAY 4: Genuine Care

DAY 5: You Before Me

MEMBERS ONE OF ANOTHER

God has a divine plan for the way His church should function. He desires that we exercise our spiritual gifts to serve one another as members of the body of Christ. In this lesson, we will learn how we can fulfill God's plan for the unity of the church by serving one another in love.

DISCUSSION

The Bible tells us that it is God who adds to the church (Acts 2:47). How and when did God bring you to this church?

Do you know or have an idea of what your spiritual gifts are? In what ways are you using them?

Have you ever done something kind for someone but with an ungracious spirit? How does the motive of love change the way in which we serve?

LESSON NOTES

WEEK ONE | DAY ONE

THE DECEPTION OF PRIDE

"For if a man think himself to be something, when he is nothing, he deceiveth himself." **GALATIANS 6:3**

It is subtle. And it is sinister. This deadly sin of pride creeps up on us and breeds an elevated perception of ourselves by inflating our ego. The very word pride has "I" in the middle—an apt depiction of self-preoccupation. Pride puts self in the center of everything and diminishes the importance of everyone else.

Have you ever let a compliment get into your head and reveled in a surge of conceit? At that moment, you might have felt good, but in reality, that pleasure was founded on deception—a false impression of your greatness. You allowed yourself to believe a lie formed in your mind.

Pride is a sin of the moment that bears eternal consequences. Remember this was the very sin that caused Satan to fall. His separation from God began with a false estimation of himself, as seen in his five conceited "I wills" in Isaiah 14:13–14: "I will ascend into heaven," "I will exalt my throne above the stars of God," "I will sit also upon the mount of the congregation, in the sides of the north," "I will ascend above the heights of the clouds," and "I will be like the most High."

The temptation to exalt our feelings and opinions always lurks within us, which is why we need to guard our hearts against entertaining any lofty illusion of ourselves. God resists the proud but gives grace to the humble (James 4:6). When we adopt an attitude of humility, we are able to see ourselves the way God does—sinners in need of a Saviour. Pride will draw us away from God, but humility will draw us toward God.

REFLECT

What did God say to me as I read today's Scripture and devotion?

RESPOND

How does this apply to my life? What actions can I take because of what I've learned?

PRAY

"Lord, forgive me for robbing You of Your glory whenever I take credit for the successes You bring. Reveal areas of pride in my life and keep me humble so that I may please You. Give me a heart that seeks to enthrone You above everything else. Amen."

WEEK ONE | DAY TWO

MORE THAN A FEELING

"By this shall all men know that ye are my disciples, if ye have love one to another." **JOHN 13:35**

Love is a word abused by overuse and misuse. The world peppers its speech with professions of "love" and reduces the meaning of love to a simplistic definition of a romantic feeling, an emotion of deep affection.

Such a diluted definition cannot hold a candle to the biblical meaning of love.

Feelings come and go. If our love for one another is only a feeling, it will be inconsistent.

Love, however, is a choice that we make daily. And it is a choice motivated by God's love for us. He first loved us and commands us to love one another (1 John 4:19–21). We love because God's love constrains, or compels, us.

Believers will stand out in an unloving world by demonstrating genuine, godly love one to another. The world will see our love and know that we are followers of Christ. The love we show serves as a marker of our identification with Christ.

Our Christian love transcends the world's shallow definition of love because it reflects God's unparalleled love for the world. And this pure, peculiar love unknown to the world is what attracts people to God.

John 3:16 tells us, "For God so loved the world…" Consider that. Then consider your love. Do you love men the way God does? Do you have a heart for a heartless world?

A love for the unlovable? Do you have a love for others that makes them see Jesus in you?

Love is an endeavor, not an emotion; it is intentional, not instinctive. Choose to love even when your feelings don't match your commitment. Choose to wear the badge of love daily as an identification with Christ. Choose to reflect the love of Christ to a world desperately in need of it.

REFLECT

What did God say to me as I read today's Scripture and devotion?

____

____

____

RESPOND

How does this apply to my life? What actions can I take because of what I've learned?

____

____

____

PRAY

"Lord, thank You for first loving me. Let Your love compel me to love others. Let others see the love of Christ in my everyday life, that they may know that I am Your disciple. Give me the strength to obey Your call to love others unconditionally. Amen."

WEEK ONE | DAY THREE

THE PURSUIT OF PEACE

"I therefore, the prisoner of the Lord, beseech you that ye walk worthy of the vocation wherewith ye are called, with all lowliness and meekness, with longsuffering, forbearing one another in love; endeavouring to keep the unity of the Spirit in the bond of peace." **EPHESIANS 4:1–3**

Put a group of people together and what do you get? Problems, usually. With the gathering of different individuals comes the potential for conflict due to clashing opinions, perspectives, and personalities. Different people have different minds, resulting in differences that cause disunity.

A hermit could live in peace away from society, but that was not God's design for man. We are not meant to live as isolated individuals, but as a cohesive community. God put believers together in the body of Christ comprised of the church.

As believers, our vocation is to follow Christ. That is our calling. And we are commanded to walk worthy of this high calling. This walk refers to our conduct or manner of life. If we call ourselves Christians, we should also live as Christians. Our speech, behavior, relationships, and attitudes ought to collectively reflect Christ.

How do we walk worthy of our calling?

Humility. Unity among the brethren begins with humility. We should esteem others better than ourselves (Philippians 2:3). Christ Himself calls us to learn of Him, for He is "meek and lowly in heart" (Matthew 11:29). To be lowly is to be emptied of self-regard.

Meekness. True strength always remains in check. It is not forceful but restrained. Meekness is a quiet strength that shuns provocation and seeks peace.

Longsuffering. If patience is an uncommon virtue in our often irritable society, longsuffering—or an enduring patience—is yet more uncommon. Human nature retaliates when offended, but longsuffering patiently bears under provocation. It is the fruit of the Spirit.

Forbearance. Similar to longsuffering, forbearance involves showing mercy on others and withholding judgment while giving people time to change. Just as God has patiently borne our deserved punishment for our sins, so we ought to forbear the flaws of others.

Endeavouring. Cultivating unity is no cakewalk, neither is preserving it. Oneness is always a work in progress, hence the use of the continuous tense in the verse. We need diligence in nurturing and maintaining the bonds of peace. And we uphold the unity of the Spirit by ministering to one another in love and seeking to serve others, not ourselves.

REFLECT

What did God say to me as I read today's Scripture and devotion?

RESPOND

How does this apply to my life? What actions can I take because of what I've learned?

PRAY

"Lord, I want to walk worthy of my calling. Help me live out my faith by pursuing peace in a world rife with strife and discord. Cultivate in me a lowly and meek spirit, patience in enduring offense and trials, and diligence in knitting the fabric of unity. Turn my self-centeredness to others-centeredness, as is becoming to a follower of Christ. Amen."

WEEK ONE | DAY FOUR

GENUINE CARE

"Let love be without dissimulation. Abhor that which is evil; cleave to that which is good. Be kindly affectioned one to another with brotherly love; in honour preferring one another." **ROMANS 12:9–10**

At a masquerade, people don masks and costumes and adopt a persona. They hide their true identities behind a performance. This is the idea behind the word *dissimulation* in Romans 12:9. It means, "hiding under a false appearance; an assumption of a counterfeit appearance which conceals real intent; hypocrisy." What you see is not what you get.

Is your love toward people an act? You might be able to feign love for a while, but it will not last. Enduring love is sincere and manifest. It is heartfelt and does not just talk, but walks in demonstrating acts of kindness. Christlike love is not a pretentious performance, but a purposed endeavor to exercise kindness to one another and put others above self. The world has no shortage of people who love and serve self. We are called to a greater love that yields to others and seeks their good over ours. When we prefer one another, everyone benefits.

Love is not all kindness and affection. It is also a hating of evil—specifically, a repugnance toward malice that harms others. When we have a genuine love for one another, we will hate evil and will be saddened when its influence reaches the family of God. We are to turn away from wickedness and hold fast to good. Do not just choose the things that are good, but embrace and pursue them relentlessly.

Today, let your love be without hypocrisy. Choose to be genuine and sensitive to others in the body of Christ.

REFLECT

What did God say to me as I read today's Scripture and devotion?

RESPOND

How does this apply to my life? What actions can I take because of what I've learned?

PRAY

"Lord, I want to love people the way You love them—with a pure, selfless heart. Give me the humility to value the good of others more than my own. Help me to reject evil, adhere to good, and love honestly. Amen."

WEEK ONE | DAY FIVE

YOU BEFORE ME

"Let nothing be done through strife or vainglory; but in lowliness of mind let each esteem other better than themselves. Look not every man on his own things, but every man also on the things of others." **PHILIPPIANS 2:3–4**

We may not admit it, but our natural bent is selfishness. It seems our three favorite people are me, myself, and I. Our flesh always seeks self over others.

We see this tendency on social media where documenting one's life becomes almost a vanity project. In our culture, we broadcast to the world what we eat, drink, play, think, and do. Then we collect "likes" on our posts, lapping up others' approval of our lives. We litter cyberspace with our comments, striving to out-shout competing voices. Every day, we jostle for our six seconds of spotlight. It is little wonder then, that humility, kindness, and selflessness have become uncommon virtues in our society.

What if we turned the tables and traded an I-first for a you-first mentality, self-centeredness for others-centeredness? This does not mean we abandon the responsibility to look after ourselves, but we value the well-being of others above our own.

Others-mindedness comes unnaturally to us. But it is the shovel that paves the way to peace and unity. Will my speech encourage or antagonize the hearer? Will my actions sow discord or concord? Putting others above self involves denial of my preferences, for sure—but it is rewarding.

When we think on the needs of others, God takes care of our needs. When we get rid of contention, we gain contentment. When we give to others, we receive satisfaction and joy.

The benefit of others will come at a cost to self. But the results will always be worth the choice.

REFLECT

What did God say to me as I read today's Scripture and devotion?

RESPOND

How does this apply to my life? What actions can I take because of what I've learned?

PRAY

"Lord, instruct me in the practice of considering others above self. Let the first person I think of be someone else, not myself. Just as You came to minister to others, use me to minister to someone today. Amen."

A NEW COMMANDMENT I GIVE UNTO YOU, THAT YE LOVE ONE ANOTHER...

JOHN 13:34

WEEK TWO

LOVE ONE ANOTHER

DAY 1: God's Definition of Love

DAY 2: Love that Glorifies God

DAY 3: The Command to Love

DAY 4: Motivations and Love

DAY 5: Love That Is Recognized by All

2

INTRODUCTION | WEEK TWO

LOVE ONE ANOTHER

Before Jesus Christ demonstrated the highest example of love on the cross, He commanded His disciples to love one another. God intended that the world would see Christ in us through our love one for another. In this lesson, we learn of Christ's love and how we are to demonstrate it toward others.

DISCUSSION

Jesus told His disciples to love one another. Who are the "one another" people in your life to whom you should show love?

What are specific ways we can "lay down our lives for the brethren" as instructed in 1 John 3:16? What would showing sacrificial love look like for you this week?

Who is a mature Christian that you look up to? In what ways do you see Christlike, sacrificial love in his or her life?

LESSON NOTES

WEEK TWO | DAY ONE

GOD'S DEFINITION OF LOVE

"Herein is love, not that we loved God, but that he loved us, and sent his Son to be the propitiation for our sins." **1 JOHN 4:10**

One of the most flippantly used words in our society is *love*. We throw around the word love to describe everything from a hamburger spot to a vacation destination. Numerous songs, television shows, and speeches have been centered on the topic of love. Couples receive attention in our society for marrying for "love"—only to end their relationships months, and sometimes even days, later. Sadly, the way society in general uses the word love makes us begin to wonder what *true* love even is.

But culture's ambiguous version of love is not biblical love. In fact, God clearly defines love in a powerful way in 1 John 4:10: "Herein is love, not that we loved God, but that he loved us, and sent his Son to be the propitiation for our sins."

Think about that verse for a few moments. Biblical love is that God sent His Son to die for us. Jesus' love for us wasn't a fickle, second guessing, in-the-moment kind of love—it was a total commitment to dying in our place so we could have eternal life. He loved us first. And, His love is constant—it doesn't change based on our actions.

May we let this incredible, emphatic, and selfless love motivate us to love and serve others today.

REFLECT

What did God say to me as I read today's Scripture and devotion?

RESPOND

How does this apply to my life? What actions can I take because of what I've learned?

PRAY

"Lord, in the busyness of life, I often find it hard to meditate on Your steadfast love for me. But, today, I choose to direct my heart and focus my thoughts on Your unconditional, faithful love. Thank You for dying for me and demonstrating that incredible love on the cross. And, thank You for the continued, daily reminders of Your love that I often fail to recognize. In my changing schedule, emotions, and thoughts—I thank You for Your love that does not change. Amen."

LOVE THAT GLORIFIES GOD

"These words spake Jesus, and lifted up his eyes to heaven, and said, Father, the hour is come; glorify thy Son, that thy Son also may glorify thee: As thou hast given him power over all flesh, that he should give eternal life to as many as thou hast given him. And this is life eternal, that they might know thee the only true God, and Jesus Christ, whom thou hast sent. I have glorified thee on the earth: I have finished the work which thou gavest me to do."
JOHN 17:1–4

Years ago, a famous violinist took center stage in a renowned concert hall. His performance that night had been widely popularized, and the hall was filled to capacity. As he finished his last song, the audience begged for an encore. The violinist played once again, his song even more beautiful than the last. Again, the audience asked for an encore. To everyone's amazement, each encore was more beautiful than the last. After several performances, the violinist finally played his last encore, bowed to the audience, and walked off the stage.

When asked why he played so many encores, he simply replied, "As I looked out at the standing audience, I noticed one person was not standing, and that was my master teacher. I played again, and still, he didn't stand. But on the last song, he finally stood. Then, I was pleased in what I had done because I had satisfied my master."[1]

Like the violinist who only sought to please his master, whom do we seek to please? Do we seek to please the world, or our Master, Jesus Christ? In the passage above,

1. "Striving to Please the Master," *Ministry 127*, http://ministry127.com/resources/illustration/striving-to-please-the-master, accessed April 28, 2019.

Jesus was expressing His ultimate goal: to glorify God. This should be our goal as well.

Do you glorify God in the way that you love others? Do your interactions with others point them to Jesus? Today, instead of focusing on pleasing others, focus on pleasing God, and watch how He changes your relationships as a result.

REFLECT

What did God say to me as I read today's Scripture and devotion?

RESPOND

How does this apply to my life? What actions can I take because of what I've learned?

PRAY

"Lord, it can be so difficult to focus on pleasing You, not others. Help me to cultivate a heart of love for You and others, seeking to glorify You in all that I do. I pray that when people see me, they will form a proper opinion of who You are. I pray that I will live my life today for Your glory alone. Amen."

WEEK TWO | DAY THREE

THE COMMAND TO LOVE

"A new commandment I give unto you, That ye love one another; as I have loved you, that ye also love one another." **JOHN 13:34**

The idea of loving others isn't just that—an idea. Nor is it even just a suggestion! In Scripture, God *commands* us to love others as He has loved us.

At first, this seems easy enough. It's easy to love our families and friends. It's easy to love people who are kind. It's easy to love people who treat us well and make us feel loved in return. But what happens when those around us aren't so easy to love? What happens when they aren't kind to us, spread rumors about us, or worse? What happens when we deal with someone who is, quite simply, unloveable?

We're still to love that person as God loved us.

You see, before we accepted Christ, we were "dead in trespasses and sins" (Ephesians 2:1). In front of a holy God, "all our righteousnesses are as filthy rags" (Isaiah 64:6). As lost sinners, nothing about us was loveable, yet Jesus still died for us. He still expressed love toward us.

He loved us at our worst. And now, He calls and commands us to demonstrate that kind of selfless love toward others.

REFLECT

What did God say to me as I read today's Scripture and devotion?

RESPOND

How does this apply to my life? What actions can I take because of what I've learned?

PRAY

"Lord, today, I thank You. Thank You for loving me at my worst. For loving me when I am unlovable. I thank You for this reminder to love like You love. Please fill me with Your Spirit and empower me to demonstrate a Christlike love to others today. I pray that through my actions, others will see Your love expressed to them. Amen."

WEEK TWO | DAY FOUR

MOTIVATIONS AND LOVE

"A new commandment I give unto you, That ye love one another; as I have loved you, that ye also love one another. By this shall all men know that ye are my disciples, if ye have love one to another." **JOHN 13:34–35**

The story is told that Hudson Taylor, the great missionary to China, once met applicants who desired to join the work in China through the China Inland Mission. He would ask them, "And why do you wish to go as a foreign missionary?"

The responses varied. Some would say, "I want to go because Christ has commanded us to go into all the world and preach the gospel to every creature." Still others would respond, "I want to go because millions are perishing without Christ."

Taylor wisely answered, "All of these motives, however good, will fail you in times of testings, trials, tribulations, and possible death. There is but one motive that will sustain you in trial and testing—namely, the love of Christ."[1]

What is your motivation behind obeying God's command to love others? Do you show love to impress those around us, almost as a performance? Do you see the command as something to check off your to do list? Or, do you love others from a heart that is motivated by the love of Christ?

God's love can transform and sustain our own expressions of love—allowing us to demonstrate a godly and unconditional love to all people God has placed in our lives. Today, let His love motivate you to serve Him by loving others selflessly and faithfully.

1. Terry Blankenship, "Our Motive for Missions" *Sermon Central*, February 9, 2009, sermoncentral.com/sermon-illustrations/72172/missions-by-sermoncentral?ref=TextIllustrationSerps.

REFLECT

What did God say to me as I read today's Scripture and devotion?

RESPOND

How does this apply to my life? What actions can I take because of what I've learned?

PRAY

"As I face this new day, Lord, I ask for the strength and purity of heart to love those around me as You have loved me. May I be motivated by Your love and may it be demonstrated to those You've placed in my life. Amen."

WEEK TWO | DAY FIVE

LOVE THAT IS RECOGNIZED BY ALL

"By this shall all men know that ye are my disciples, if ye have love one to another." **JOHN 13:35**

In the nineteenth century, a famous atheist named Charles Bradlaugh challenged a Christian pastor named Hugh Price Hughes to a debate. Bradlaugh's plan was to go head-to-head against Hughes and prove that Christianity simply had no valid foundation. Hughes accepted with a condition of his own. He said, "Before we debate, I want you to bring one hundred people whose lives have been transformed by atheism. I will also bring one hundred people whose lives have been transformed by Jesus."

Hughes continued, "If, upon looking for one hundred, you find it impossible, you may bring fifty. And if you can't find fifty, you may bring twenty. In fact, if you bring just one person whose life has been transformed through atheism, I can bring one hundred people whose lives have been transformed by the power of the gospel." As a result, Bradlaugh declined to debate.[1] Hughes recognized a powerful truth: the gospel changes lives and has a transforming impact on the lost world.

The transforming power of the gospel in our lives cannot be understated! We praise God that He changed us—made us new creatures—at the time of our salvation. This difference is meant to be seen by others. The man who, before he met Christ, didn't show love is now sensitive in his treatment of others. The woman who, before she met Christ, was rude in her speech, is now loving in her words and actions. The transforming power of the gospel is evidenced by our loving actions toward each other!

1. Paul Lee Tan, *Encyclopedia of 7,700 Illustrations* (McDonald, TN: Assurance Publishers, 1979).

So, how is your testimony? Do your neighbors and coworkers know that Christ has changed your life? Our testimonies are one of the greatest tools we have as we share God's love and reach a lost world with the gospel. May we use it wisely today!

REFLECT

What did God say to me as I read today's Scripture and devotion?

RESPOND

How does this apply to my life? What actions can I take because of what I've learned?

PRAY

"Lord, I want to be a testimony to those around me—pointing others to You. Please let my actions please you and reflect You to my family, friends, and coworkers. Help my love for You and others to grow, along with my desire to live righteously. Let all those who look at my life clearly see my love for You in everything I do. Amen."

LET THE WORD OF CHRIST DWELL IN YOU RICHLY IN ALL WISDOM; TEACHING AND ADMONISHING ONE ANOTHER...

COLOSSIANS 3:16

WEEK THREE

ADMONISH ONE ANOTHER

DAY 1: In My Heart, on My Lips

DAY 2: Meditate for Success

DAY 3: Music as a Means of Admonishment

DAY 4: A Teacher of Truth

DAY 5: Receiving Admonition with Grace

3

ADMONISH ONE ANOTHER

Do you resent being reproved? Or are you indifferent to admonishing someone who needs it? In this study, we learn that God wants His Word to dwell richly in our lives and for us to teach and admonish one another according to His Word.

DISCUSSION

What are the regular ways you are hearing and receiving Scripture? How can you increase your intake of it?

What is the most helpful method you have found for memorizing Scripture?

What are a few spiritual or life topics in which you wish you knew more Scripture to be able to teach or admonish others? Where could you begin in studying those topics?

LESSON NOTES

WEEK THREE | DAY ONE

IN MY HEART, ON MY LIPS

"Let the word of Christ dwell in you richly in all wisdom..." COLOSSIANS 3:16

George Müller was a busy man. It is estimated that, for forty years, he penned 30,000 letters each year. He headed five orphanages, supervised a publishing company, and pastored a church of 1,200. His testimony of faith in God has encouraged countless Christians. But there was one thing Müller prioritized, and that was the Bible. Of God's Word, Müller said, "I never think of going to my work without first having a good season of time with God and my Bible."

God used George Müller to kindly and compassionately admonish thousands of believers through his orphanages, church, and other ministry endeavors. His powerful testimony speaks to many believers, and it made a lasting impact because he was committed to God's Word.

Before we're able to admonish one another, as the last lesson reminded us, we must first ensure that God's Word dwells in our hearts. That word *dwell* implies something that is settled down or is at home. How can we practically allow God's Word to abide in us? Consider these actions, covered in this week's lesson:

- **Listen**—Be an attentive listener to Scripture as it is shared, taught, and preached. Let God's Word take root in your heart as you absorb its truths. Consider starting a Bible reading plan or commit to being faithful to church and to opportunities to hear God's Word.

- **Study**—Beyond hearing and reading, study the Bible for truth and application. Become a student of Scripture, rightly dividing and discerning its life-changing principles. You may want to do a Bible word study or keep an ongoing journal of truths that God reveals to you.

- **Memorize**— Scripture memorization is a key component to allowing God's Word to dwell in us. Effectively admonishing others in God's Word will also involve committing portions of Scripture to memory, so that from your heart, you can communicate truths you've learned personally. Write out God's Word or use an app or method to memorize it, even as you go about your day.

- **Share**—As you speak God's Word to others, you'll experience greater reinforcement of its truths in your life and you will admonish and encourage others at the same time. Determine who you can share God's Word with, starting in your own home and with opportunities given to you by God through your local church.

May the word of Christ dwell in you this week, and may you glean from the riches of its beautiful wisdom!

REFLECT

What did God say to me as I read today's Scripture and devotion?

RESPOND

How does this apply to my life? What actions can I take because of what I've learned?

PRAY

"Lord, I want to prioritize Your Word in my life. Please speak to me through Your Word, and let it flow through me as a source of help and blessing to others. Let me speak Your truth rather than my opinions, and allow me to encourage and lovingly admonish those You've put in my path this week. Amen."

WEEK THREE | DAY TWO

MEDITATE FOR SUCCESS

"This book of the law shall not depart out of thy mouth; but thou shalt meditate therein day and night, that thou mayest observe to do according to all that is written therein: for then thou shalt make thy way prosperous, and then thou shalt have good success." **JOSHUA 1:8**

You may know that cows have a unique way of digesting their food. When they first eat, they are unable to get all of the nutrition needed from it, so they re-chew their food a second time. This process of "chewing the cud" is known as ruminating. The same word is also used to indicate carefully thinking on something, or, as the expression goes, "chewing something over."

This same approach—of carefully thinking on something—is one we should use with Scripture. We meditate and analyze all the time—just not always on God and His Word. It takes a conscious choice and determination to meditate on Scripture. But when we do, God promises to give success in every aspect of life, including our relationships.

Identify ways in which you can actively meditate on God's Word this week. Here are a few examples to get you started:

- Write out portions of Scripture.
- Place verses where you will see them often.
- Pray the Scriptures.
- Sing Scripture songs.
- Listen to an audio version of the Bible as you go throughout your day.

Meditating on Scripture is vitally important to our personal spiritual growth in developing a strong foundation for success in life. Saturating our minds with God's Word also allows us to strengthen and develop meaningful interactions with others as we seek to admonish and encourage each other in the Lord.

REFLECT

What did God say to me as I read today's Scripture and devotion?

RESPOND

How does this apply to my life? What actions can I take because of what I've learned?

PRAY

"Lord, I acknowledge my desperate need for Your truth in my life. Without Your truth, I cannot succeed, and without Your truth, I cannot effectively encourage others. Show me what You want me to learn from Your Word, and help me to meditate on it throughout this day. May "...the words of my mouth, and the meditation of my heart, be acceptable in thy sight, O Lord, my strength, and my redeemer" (Psalm 19:14). Amen."

MUSIC AS A MEANS OF ADMONISHMENT

"Let the word of Christ dwell in you richly in all wisdom; teaching and admonishing one another in psalms and hymns and spiritual songs, singing with grace in your hearts to the Lord." **COLOSSIANS 3:16**

It's happened to all of us. We've had a song stuck in our head—maybe annoyingly so, in the sense that we cannot seem to shake the tune or lyrics from our minds. Maybe it's gone on for hours or even days before dissipating...only for a friend to quietly whistle its tune as the whole process begins again in our minds!

The power of music is amazing. Perhaps you've never thought much (at least not before this lesson) about music as a powerful means of admonishment in your relationships. How wonderful to know that God created music with one of the purposes being the teaching and encouraging of fellow Christians!

In the passage we're studying this week, God is instructing us to use the gift of music to reinforce the truths of His Word in the hearts of believers. If you're going to be singing or thinking or repeating words throughout this week—what better lyrics than the beautiful words of Scripture!

Music should glorify God and ascribe worth to Him. It can help us remember who He is and what He can do. And, it also enables us to teach and admonish others through its memorable arrangements of lyrics and words.

So—sing! Join in congregational worship. Teach your children a Bible song. Share an encouraging and Scriptural song with a friend. Listen to Christ-honoring music throughout your day. Worship God, and reinforce His Word in your heart this week.

REFLECT

What did God say to me as I read today's Scripture and devotion?

RESPOND

How does this apply to my life? What actions can I take because of what I've learned?

PRAY

"Thank You, God, for the gift of music. Thank You for the opportunity to use it as a source of worship to You and encouragement for myself and others. I choose to praise You from the heart this week by singing psalms, hymns, and spiritual songs. Please help me as I seek to glorify You through this form of worship and instruction. Amen."

A TEACHER OF TRUTH

"All Scripture is given by inspiration of God, and is profitable for doctrine, for reproof, for correction, for instruction in righteousness." **2 TIMOTHY 3:16**

When you hear the word *teacher*, what is the first thought or memory that comes to mind? A grumpy high school teacher? An influential elementary teacher? Do you picture someone standing at a lectern delivering a less-than-interesting monologue?

In today's passage, God calls all of us to be *gracious* teachers and communicators of His Word. He wants us to be knowledgeable teachers to edify one another in His Word, and to be humble, receptive students when others admonish us.

As we communicate God's Word to other believers and listen as it is taught to us, an obvious goal is to impart biblical *instruction*. Second Timothy 3 reminds us that God's Word is profitable for instruction—teaching us how to live our daily lives.

Another purpose for teaching God's Word is to develop grounded believers. As we grow in our own understanding of Scripture, we can communicate truth to those growing in their faith and biblical *discernment*.

Sharing God's Word with others also involves the goal of *encouragement*. As a teacher of the Bible, you have the opportunity to offer great hope and comfort found in the pages of Scripture.

As you think of teachers from your past or present, you may or may not identify with them in their style, approach, delivery, or content. But, as a believer, you've been given the role of "teacher" by God Himself. Whether or not you feel qualified for the task, He promises to enable and fill you. So, who can you teach today? Look for opportunities to share God's Word with your children. Volunteer to participate in the sharing of truth through the ministries of your church. Share the Good News of salvation with others, teaching them the way to eternal life. Ask God for a creative idea and fresh perspective, and just get started!

God can and desires to use *you* to teach others! What a beautiful thought and sacred responsibility. Claim His strength and step out in purpose to communicate His Word this week.

REFLECT

What did God say to me as I read today's Scripture and devotion?

RESPOND

How does this apply to my life? What actions can I take because of what I've learned?

PRAY

"Lord, as I seek to grow in my knowledge of You and Your Word, I want to also grow in my encouragement and admonishment to others. Use me as a teacher of truth, and help me faithfully share it at every opportunity You provide—whether big or small—realizing the significance of both, as You promise that your Word will not return void. I pray for grace and humility, wisdom and discernment, peace and boldness as a communicator for You. Amen."

WEEK THREE | DAY FIVE

RECEIVING ADMONITION WITH GRACE

"Iron sharpeneth iron; so a man sharpeneth the countenance of his friend."
PROVERBS 27:17

In your kitchen, you likely have a selection of kitchen knives. When one needs sharpening, the most common method is to apply pressure and friction to one knife with the other. In doing so, both objects are sharpened.

God created our relationships with this same sharpening effect. He desires that in grace, we share and receive admonition. While it at times might feel uncomfortable and may involve some pressure or even friction—God calls us to move past these hindrances so that from a pure and sincere heart, we can sharpen each other.

When our walk with the Lord begins to weaken or we begin to struggle in a specific area, a friend in Christ can come alongside us with an encouraging verse or gentle reminder. God may use a timely sermon to bring conviction. He may use a friend's quiet, biblical comment to surprisingly align your heart to His will. Regardless of the delivery, these loving admonishments, when given with grace and truth, are designed by God to make you stronger and sharper in your Christian life.

Generally, admonition is not something we particularly enjoy. Correction is rarely fun or inviting. It exposes our weaknesses and can often hurt our pride. But the passage we've studied this week gives us permission to see admonition from a fresh perspective! Instead of an embarrassment or frustration, loving admonishment from Spirit-filled sources can be a gift! Admonition is an opportunity to grow in the Lord and strengthen your relationship with Him and others.

As this week concludes and you prepare your heart for the next group study, take a moment to ask the Holy Spirit to soften your heart to biblical admonition. Strive to be a gracious recipient when truth is spoken into your life. Ask God to remove any barriers to truth that you've built in your heart, and thank Him for the gift of sharpening relationships!

REFLECT

What did God say to me as I read today's Scripture and devotion?

RESPOND

How does this apply to my life? What actions can I take because of what I've learned?

PRAY

"God, while admonishment doesn't always feel like a gift, I thank you for the blessing of admonishment in my life. Thank You for caring enough about my spiritual growth to send messengers of truth to speak Your Word to me. I pray that as I hear needed and biblical counsel, I will be graciously receptive and willing to change and grow. Please give me wisdom and strength to live a truly humble and moldable life for Your glory. Amen."

...USE NOT LIBERTY FOR AN OCCASION TO THE FLESH, BUT BY LOVE SERVE ONE ANOTHER.

GALATIANS 5:13

WEEK FOUR

SERVE ONE ANOTHER

DAY 1: The Gift of Salvation

DAY 2: Living by Grace

DAY 3: Liberty and Responsibility

DAY 4: Loving Before Serving

DAY 5: The Service of Prayer

4

SERVE ONE ANOTHER

One of the blessings we enjoy as Christians is the liberty we have in Christ. We are freed from the bondage and guilt of sin and given liberty to follow God. This liberty was paid for with Christ's blood, and it is a precious gift. This is not a gift, however, to selfishly squander. It is, rather, a gift to be used to serve one another. In this study, we learn what Christian liberty is and how God intended for us to exercise our freedom in Christ.

DISCUSSION

Serving others helps us break the tendency of being self-focused. What are some indicators you've noticed in your life that point to a need to break out of self-focus?

What are some of the common burdens, experiences, events, or needs during which people especially need to be served? Do you know anyone in your church family right now who is in any of those situations?

What practical ways have you found to organize your prayer list or your prayer time to regularly pray for the needs of others?

LESSON NOTES

WEEK FOUR | DAY ONE

THE GIFT OF SALVATION

"I do not frustrate the grace of God: for if righteousness come by the law, then Christ is dead in vain." **GALATIANS 2:21**

Imagine someone presented you a gift. Touched and delighted, you open it to discover that it's just the gift you've always wanted. You express your thanks to the giver. He then tells you it's only yours to keep only if you do a list of things for him. How would you feel? That "gift" wasn't quite a gift, because it came attached with a string of conditions.

When God presented us the gift of salvation, He gave it freely. All you had to do was receive it. That is a gift in the true sense of the word. It is free because God had already paid for it and does not require any work on our part. If salvation can be earned, it ceases to be a gift. Christ's death on the cross would have been in vain if our good works could save us.

Religion tells us "do." God tells us "done." His work on the cross is final and our salvation is complete in Him. Have you struggled with your salvation because you felt you kept failing Him? Look to the cross. Your past, present, and future sins have been dealt with at Calvary.

If you've never completely relied on Christ for salvation, today is a great day to make that choice. Instead of trusting in your righteousness or good works, rely on Christ. And, if you've already made that choice, choose to share the good news of the gift of salvation with the world around you.

Our world is searching for peace with God, but they often completely miss what true salvation is. They think they have to do something to earn salvation. It is our privilege as Christians to share with a lost world the news that salvation is a gift they can't earn but simply receive.

REFLECT

What did God say to me as I read today's Scripture and devotion?

RESPOND

How does this apply to my life? What actions can I take because of what I've learned?

PRAY

"Lord, thank You for the gift of salvation. Thank You for paying the price I could never pay. Help me to rest in Your complete work and share this gift with a lost and dying world. Amen."

WEEK FOUR | DAY TWO

LIVING BY GRACE

"But by the grace of God I am what I am: and his grace which was bestowed upon me was not in vain; but I laboured more abundantly than they all: yet not I, but the grace of God which was with me." **1 CORINTHIANS 15:10**

John Newton, the author of "Amazing Grace," is the last person you'd have thought would come to know Christ. He was an immoral slave trader who was also known as "The Great Blasphemer." But God's grace changed him one day. After his salvation, he penned many beloved hymns rich in biblical significance.

Newton understood what an incredible gift God's grace is. He said, "I am not what I might be, I am not what I ought to be, I am not what I wish to be, I am not what I hope to be. But I thank God I am not what I once was, and I can say with the great apostle, 'By the grace of God I am what I am.'" Living the Christian life, as Newton recognized, has nothing to do with our performance and everything to do with growing in grace. Newton knew that he had many areas in his life in which he needed to grow. Yet he also recognized the power of God's grace, not as an excuse to continue in sin, but as an agent of change in his life to grow as a Christian.

As Christians, we understand that we're saved by faith in Christ, not by our works or our performance. But sometimes, we can get so wrapped up in trying to do right after salvation that we turn it into a performance, not a life guided by grace. Before we can truly serve others, we have to stand fast in our position as Christians. We have to realize that whatever we do for Christ must be fueled out of a love for God and His grace working in our lives. Nothing that we do can make God love us any more. The secret to a fulfilled life as a Christian is to allow Christ to work in and through us.

REFLECT

What did God say to me as I read today's Scripture and devotion?

RESPOND

How does this apply to my life? What actions can I take because of what I've learned?

PRAY

"Lord, help to never forget that, just as I'm saved by grace, I also live by grace. I want to serve You out of a heart of love, not of performance. Help me to stand fast in the liberty You offered at salvation, secure in the identity You've given me. And from that place of rest and security, give me the strength and wisdom to serve You and others today and throughout this week. Amen."

WEEK FOUR | DAY THREE

LIBERTY AND RESPONSIBILITY

"For, brethren, ye have been called unto liberty; only use not liberty for an occasion to the flesh, but by love serve one another." **GALATIANS 5:13**

Do you remember when you first got your driver's license? You must have felt a great sense of newfound freedom. Seated behind the driver's wheel, you could go anywhere you wanted, whenever you wanted.

With that great freedom came responsibility. There were traffic rules to follow, and speed limits to observe. If you beat a red light, you get a ticket. If you drink and drive, you get arrested. The rules were in place to keep you safe, and so long as you abided by them, you could enjoy your freedom to drive.

It's the same with grace. Being in Christ means that we have freedom—we're no longer under the bondage of sin. While we do not follow a set of rules to earn our salvation, we do have a responsibility to serve Christ and to keep His commandments, which are meant for our good.

Paul cautioned the believers in Galatia not to use their Christian liberty as an occasion to the flesh. By this, he meant that it's wrong to use our freedom in Christ as an excuse to continue in sin. In fact, because we're in Christ, we have the Holy Spirit in us, enabling us to live righteously and claim victory over the sin we struggle with.

Let grace motivate you to draw closer to the Lord this week, living a life that pleases Him. When we truly recognize what grace-fueled Christianity is, we'll live lives of love and service that please the Lord and bless others.

REFLECT

What did God say to me as I read today's Scripture and devotion?

RESPOND

How does this apply to my life? What actions can I take because of what I've learned?

PRAY

"Lord, I'm so thankful for Your gift of grace, not just for salvation, but to live the Christian life. Please help me to use this grace, not as an excuse to continue in sin, but to draw closer to You. I claim Your grace to live soberly, righteously, and godly this week. Amen."

WEEK FOUR | DAY FOUR

LOVING BEFORE SERVING

"And thou shalt love the Lord thy God with all thy heart, and with all thy soul, and with all thy mind, and with all thy strength: this is the first commandment. And the second is like, namely this, Thou shalt love thy neighbor as thyself. There is none other commandment greater than these."
MARK 12:30–31

Imagine a perfectly still, smooth lake. Now, picture picking up a small rock and throwing it as far as you can into the center of the lake. Soon, you see ripples spreading out across the water from where the little rock landed. The size of the rock did not matter in creating a ripple effect—it was simply the fact that the rock was used.

God wants us to make an impact on others. And He is not looking at our accomplishments to do the job, but at our availability. He seeks Christians with willing hearts to serve Him. If you are available for His service, He wants to use you!

Just as the small rock affected a large lake when it was thrown, any Christian in the hands of God can make a significant impact on other believers...and on the world.

So then, what will motivate us to serve God—to be available for His purposes? A love for Him. And when we love the Lord, He will give us a love for others, along with a heart to serve them. When we love Him with all our heart, soul, mind, and strength, serving Him and serving others becomes a delight, not a duty—a joy, not a burden.

Today, may we remember that God wants our hearts before He wants our service. It doesn't matter to Him what size rock we are! When we place our hearts in His hands, He can use us to make a significant difference for eternity!

REFLECT

What did God say to me as I read today's Scripture and devotion?

RESPOND

How does this apply to my life? What actions can I take because of what I've learned?

PRAY

"Lord, at times I feel insignificant—as if my efforts to serve You make no impact at all. But, then, I am reminded of what is most important—what is the greatest commandment. And that is to simply love You. Please help me as I cultivate a greater love for You. Grow my love for You. And from this place of love, please use my service for You to make a great difference in the lives of others, I pray. Amen."

WEEK FOUR | DAY FIVE

THE SERVICE OF PRAYER

"Praying always with all prayer and supplication in the Spirit, and watching thereunto with all perseverance and supplication for all saints;"
EPHESIANS 6:18

There are times when the needs of a fellow Christian are simply beyond our means of help: the grief of losing a loved one, the suffering of an incurable disease, or the hurt of a spouse's unfaithfulness. When we find ourselves at the end of our resources to help another, remember, the first and best resource is always available to us—prayer.

Even behind bars, the apostle Paul continued to minister to the Philippian believers by praying that their love for God would continue to grow (Philippians 1:3–9). Prison was not an obstacle to his ministry, but an opportunity for prayer.

When the church learned of Peter's imprisonment, they gathered for a prayer meeting (Acts 12:5). Powerless to release him, they relied on the power of prayer. They could not make a way of escape for Peter, but they believed in a God who could—and He did. James 5:16 tells us: "The effectual fervent prayer of a righteous man availeth much."

When you have a heart to help and serve, but feel you don't know what to do or where to start—start with prayer. Prayer is a wonderful, powerful way to serve and minister to the needs of others.

What a beautiful and reassuring truth that prayer can make a difference! May we pray for others this week with fervency and perseverance, trusting God to meet needs in miraculous ways.

REFLECT

What did God say to me as I read today's Scripture and devotion?

RESPOND

How does this apply to my life? What actions can I take because of what I've learned?

PRAY

"Lord, at times I feel limited in my ability to help and serve others during seasons of grief, pain, loss, or trial. Like Paul, help me to see my limitations as an opportunity to pray rather than obstacles to overcome. Thank You for Your promise that my fervent prayers on behalf of others are the most effective means of serving them. I lift up those who are hurting today. Amen."

LET NO CORRUPT COMMUNICATION PROCEED OUT OF YOUR MOUTH, BUT THAT WHICH IS GOOD TO THE USE OF EDIFYING...

EPHESIANS 4:29

WEEK FIVE

BE KIND TO ONE ANOTHER

DAY 1: Be Angry and Sin Not

DAY 2: Anger Danger

DAY 3: Kindness Like Confetti

DAY 4: Kindness in Action

DAY 5: Kind on Purpose

5

BE KIND TO ONE ANOTHER

We live in an angry world filled with hatred and bitterness. Are we as Christians contributing to this mess, or are we making a difference by communicating kindness to a world that is hurting? Today, we look at what kindness is and learn the ways we can communicate it to one another.

DISCUSSION

What sins have you seen that often accompany anger?

What is the kindest thing someone has said to you? What made it so memorable? And how could you pass it on to someone else?

Why do you think it is often easier to show kindness to strangers while overlooking those closest to us? To whom in your life do you need to purposefully show regular kindness?

LESSON NOTES

WEEK FIVE | DAY ONE

BE ANGRY AND SIN NOT

"Be ye angry, and sin not: let not the sun go down upon your wrath."
EPHESIANS 4:26

The focus of this week's lesson is kindness. We studied that the opposing emotion to kindness is anger. Emotions of anger and frustration conflict with the kindness and grace God commands us to demonstrate to one another.

God created us with emotions, and we all experience some form of anger. Yet, anger in itself isn't necessarily wrong. We read in the gospels of Jesus Himself expressing anger. So, what is the biblical perspective? Anger becomes a sin when it is directed toward a person who offends instead of toward a sin problem that needs a solution.

As we focus our hearts on personally experiencing God's peace and then demonstrating a Christlike kindness to others, it's helpful to realize that frustration in relationships is primarily a sin problem, not a people problem. Acknowledging this is a key step toward finding a solid solution of dealing with sin rather than attacking a person.

If you are experiencing anger in your relationships, ask God for wisdom in dealing with the root, sin issues. Determine to focus on God's solution for the sin problem, and ask God to help you love the person with whom the conflict arises.

And, as the second portion of this verse reminds us, don't let time pass without making things right with God and others. Keep short accounts; strive to live peaceably with all men. Commit to pursuing peace in your relationships by confessing sin and praying for yourself and others.

God promises to bless our relationships when we commit to demonstrating kindness toward others, hatred only for sin, and love for the body of Christ. May God bless you with grace and peace as you seek to please Him in your interactions with others today.

REFLECT

What did God say to me as I read today's Scripture and devotion?

RESPOND

How does this apply to my life? What actions can I take because of what I've learned?

PRAY

"God, I come before you today acknowledging my need for Your peace in my relationships. I pray that any feelings of relational frustration or anger will drive me to You for the strength to deal with sin and demonstrate kindness to those You love. Please give me courage to address any issues right away, as I seek to keep a heart that is always right with You and those You've placed in my life. Thank You for being my perfect example, my source of strength and wisdom. I claim Your power to live a life that is pleasing to You today. Amen."

ANGER DANGER

"Wherefore, my beloved brethren, let every man be swift to hear, slow to speak, slow to wrath: For the wrath of man worketh not the righteousness of God." **JAMES 1:19-20**

Billy Sunday was a great preacher of the nineteenth and twentieth centuries. He saw many come to know Christ and countless lives changed through his preaching. One day, he spoke to a woman who dealt with anger issues. She brushed off her struggle, saying, "There's nothing wrong with losing my temper. I blow up, and then it's all over." "So does a shotgun," Sunday wisely responded, "and look at the damage it leaves behind!"[1]

When there is an explosion of anger in our lives, our relationships are always in danger. Sadly, the damage anger causes is sometimes so significant, we often carry the broken pieces and unresolved conflict for years. Its consequences can have a serious, negative impact on our relationships with others and with the Lord.

There are three obvious dangers that come as a result of anger expressed toward others:

Unresolved anger can cause us to react prematurely. In the heat of the moment, anger does not pause. It does not think. It reacts irrationally and afterward, brings regret. But the Bible gives us a caution in James 1:19: "Wherefore, my beloved brethren, let every man be swift to hear, slow to speak, slow to wrath."

Unresolved anger can damage our testimonies. Anger can start small—maybe a clipped tone toward a co-worker or a pointed look toward a family member. But

1. Bill Bright and Henry Brandt, *Soul Prescription* (Enumclaw, WA: Pleasant Word, 2009).

if we allow that anger to remain in our spirits, it slowly grows, hurting others and negatively affecting our testimonies. It is so vital to deal with anger *before* it impacts our relationships.

Anger gives place to the devil. The devil looks for any opportunity to get a foothold in our lives, and anger is one of his most used entry points. When we're angry, he takes advantage of the moment, causing us to do and say things we never initially considered. As Ephesians 4 challenges, don't give Satan this opportunity! Stay strong in the Spirit, allowing Him to cultivate a heart of peace in all situations.

As Christians, may we not dismiss anger as a trivial issue to accept or ignore. May we recognize the danger it poses to our God-given friendships, and may we choose to respond in kindness in the power of the Holy Spirit.

REFLECT

What did God say to me as I read today's Scripture and devotion?

RESPOND

How does this apply to my life? What actions can I take because of what I've learned?

PRAY

"Lord, it's often my natural tendency to respond in the flesh and react in anger when I am hurt. Thank You for showing me the danger that can occur as I allow unresolved anger to foster in my heart. Help me as I seek to genuinely love others. Please give me grace to show kindness so that I can positively make a difference in Your kingdom for years to come. Amen."

KINDNESS LIKE CONFETTI

"Death and life are in the power of the tongue: and they that love it shall eat the fruit thereof." **PROVERBS 18:21**

Have you noticed the emphasis placed on kindness in many aspects of our modern society? Maybe you've seen the shirt that says, *In a world where you can be anything, be kind*. Or you might have seen a phone case or water bottle with the label, *Throw kindness around like confetti*. Even a culture contrary to most biblical principles recognizes the importance of kindness.

For the Christian, however, kindness is not a cliché or just an important virtue. It is also a direct command from the Lord. And, sometimes obeying the biblical command is a little more complicated than throwing confetti. It involves Holy Spirit empowerment and enabling.

As we consider our speech, we'd probably (sadly) admit that it's easy to throw around words of gossip, hurt, doubt, or lies. They sometimes slip out before we even realize the significance of what is happening! But, to pour words of life, truth, empathy, compassion, and kindness into someone takes intention, discernment, and wisdom.

The words of Proverbs 18:21 serve as a powerful reminder: you have the ability to change a life or to wound a spirit. Just one remark—one word—can tear someone down or lift someone up to walk in the purpose God has given them.

Kindness is a powerful tool. It is often expressed by the words we say. So, why not? Go ahead and spread God's love like confetti. Speak His love to your family and friends today. Bless them with His words of comfort and truth. Speak life to them. Be a living, communicative demonstration of God's kindness today.

REFLECT

What did God say to me as I read today's Scripture and devotion?

RESPOND

How does this apply to my life? What actions can I take because of what I've learned?

PRAY

"Heavenly Father, I admit that speaking without thinking is so easy. I often don't realize the negative impact my speech can have on others. Help me to be intentional in my speech—pointing others to You and speaking the truth in love. Help me to build people up, not tear them down. I pray that Christ-honoring speech will flow from my heart and mouth today in a way that will bless and encourage others. Please use me as an agent for kindness to those needing encouragement. Amen."

WEEK FIVE | DAY FOUR

KINDNESS IN ACTION

"Put on therefore, as the elect of God, holy and beloved, bowels of mercies, kindness, humbleness of mind, meekness, longsuffering;" **COLOSSIANS 3:12**

They are easy to spot. With flip flops, sunglasses, a big hat, and even bigger camera—you can identify the stereotypical tourist from a mile away. (You may even admit that you've been that stereotypical tourist a time or two!)

It's also not hard to identify different professions based on the attire and characteristics of their daily living—Business professionals wear suits and go to meetings in high rise buildings. Chefs wear tall hats and white aprons with their creativity coming to life in a hot and busy kitchen. Conductors wear black tuxes, carry conductors' wands, and unite groups of people to play beautiful music.

Just as characteristics such as these describe a group of people or a profession or person—kindness is always characterized by certain behaviors and actions.

As Christians seeking to edify one another, do our actions speak of love and kindness? Do we possess defining characteristics that prove our Christlike affection for each other?

How do we know? What does kindness in action look like? We looked at a few of these qualities from Ephesians 4 in our group study, but as we prayerfully consider the changes God would have us implement, let's revisit these characteristics:

Kindness is gentle. We can sometimes equate gentleness with weakness, but the reality is that being gentle often requires tremendous strength. It involves meekness, even in the middle of conflict, and a Christlike manner and approach to all situations and people.

Kindness is compassionate. Compassion has been described as "feeling your hurt in my heart." We never know what others are going through, but a kind heart chooses to be compassionate when a situation might otherwise be irritating. Maybe the rude grocery clerk just received a bad doctor's report. Perhaps the angry customer is going through a divorce. God can enable us to consider others and respond with compassion by feeling their hurts in our hearts.

So—can you be spotted a mile away, not because of your physical characteristics, but because of your spiritual actions? Do you treat others with gentleness? Do you have a godly empathy and compassion for others? Do you demonstrate this through your actions?

To whom can you show kindness, and how would kindness be best expressed? Never resist the Holy Spirit's promptings to put kindness in action. You won't regret it.

REFLECT

What did God say to me as I read today's Scripture and devotion?

RESPOND

How does this apply to my life? What actions can I take because of what I've learned?

PRAY

"Lord, help me to put kindness in action today. As I consider your incredible kindness expressed to me on a daily basis, please help me to share that with others. Please give me a heart to be kind one to another as You've taught in Your Word. I ask for Your perspective as I look to meet the needs of others by actions of kindness and love. Help others to see You through me. Amen."

KIND ON PURPOSE

"And be ye kind one to another, tenderhearted, forgiving one another, even as God for Christ's sake hath forgiven you." **EPHESIANS 4:32**

The kindest person who ever walked on this earth was Jesus Christ. With purpose given to Him from His Heavenly Father, He healed the sick, fed the hungry, gave sight to the blind. He listened. He loved. He taught. He forgave.

You, too, have been called to intentional, purposeful kindness. As Christ has forgiven you, you have been commanded to forgive others, demonstrating a sacrificial, active love and showing a kind, tender heart toward one another.

If you need motivation—look to the cross, where Jesus performed the greatest act of kindness in the history of mankind by dying to pay the price for your sin.

If you need inspiration—read the Gospels and learn from His example. Study how He spoke to the outcast, spent time with the unpopular, and loved everyone.

If you need strength—ask Him to empower and enable you to communicate His kindness to those He leads to you.

Being kind doesn't happen by accident. It doesn't happen by chance. It requires intentional effort and Holy Spirit filling. It takes a heart purposed to obey and choosing to love. Kindness happens on purpose. And, it's *your* purpose. With God's help, fulfill that purpose today!

REFLECT

What did God say to me as I read today's Scripture and devotion?

RESPOND

How does this apply to my life? What actions can I take because of what I've learned?

PRAY

"Lord, I stand in awe of the kindness You expressed to me on the cross of Calvary. Thank You for providing such an example of love and forgiveness. Please help me to walk in Your steps today, choosing to purposefully demonstrate kindness to others. Fill me with Your Spirit as I seek to fulfill Your purposes for my life today. Amen."

AND BE YE KIND
ONE TO ANOTHER,
TENDERHEARTED,
FORGIVING ONE
ANOTHER...

EPHESIANS 4:32

WEEK SIX

FORGIVE ONE ANOTHER

DAY 1: The Manifestation of Anger

DAY 2: A Message of Reconciliation

DAY 3: Anger Bombs

DAY 4: Seeking Revenge or Pursuing Peace

DAY 5: Forgive as Christ Forgave

6

FORGIVE ONE ANOTHER

Every one of us has had to seek forgiveness at some point in our lives because of our mistakes. While we are eager to receive forgiveness, we find it hard to forgive someone who has wronged us. God commands us to forgive others unconditionally because He has done the same for us. When we forgive, our relationships are restored, and we bring healing to our lives.

DISCUSSION

What negative "side effects" have you observed in the lives of others (or yourself) who become consumed with bitterness?

What positive "side effects" have you noticed in your own life when you have chosen to forgive someone?

Where and when did you receive God's forgiveness through Christ?

LESSON NOTES

WEEK SIX | DAY ONE

THE MANIFESTATION OF ANGER

"Then said Jesus, Father, forgive them; for they know not what they do."
LUKE 23:34

In hopes of securing a place in Heaven, Phuljharia Kunwar, came up with an elaborate plan. She invited 100,000 people to a massive feast. For two days, she fed everyone in the surrounding villages, spending an estimated $37,500.

Her goal was to ultimately gain favor with the gods and an entrance into Heaven.[1] Sadly, what Phulijharia failed to realize was that forgiveness and salvation have nothing to do with what we spend and everything to do with what *He* gave.

In our world, some will go to elaborate lengths in hope of earning Heaven. They feel the overwhelming need to earn forgiveness from God.

Forgiveness from Christ has nothing to do with our effort. In fact, it starts with simply recognizing our need for it. You see, God is a just God. When we sin, He can't just overlook what we've done. But God is also a loving God. He doesn't want us to suffer in Hell, so He sent His Son to take our place. Because Jesus died for us, we have a way to be reconciled to God.

As Jesus suffered on the cross, He said, "Father, forgive them; for they know not what they do" (Luke 23:34). These are incredible words! Jesus forgave us of our sin, not because we're worthy, but because He loved us.

Throughout this week, we will focus on offering forgiveness when it does not feel natural or fair. But it is important to remember that true forgiveness comes from

1. Bappa Majumdar, "Widow throws party to find place in heaven, *Reuters*, June 6, 2008, https://www.reuters.com/article/us-widow-feast/widow-throws-party-to-find-place-in-heaven-idUSDEL27714220080606.

those who have first been forgiven. We can't extend God's love to others if we don't first know it ourselves.

If you have not accepted God's gift of forgiveness for your sins, get that settled today by acknowledging your need and placing your faith in Christ alone. And if you have received His forgiveness, thank God for such a miraculous gift and offer His forgiveness to others in your life!

REFLECT

What did God say to me as I read today's Scripture and devotion?

RESPOND

How does this apply to my life? What actions can I take because of what I've learned?

PRAY

"God, thank You for sending Your Son to die in my place. I'm so glad that my salvation isn't contingent on anything that I do, but completely on You and what You've done for me. I want to rest in that today and focus on the incredible gift of forgiveness You have offered to me. Amen."

WEEK SIX | DAY TWO

A MESSAGE OF RECONCILIATION

"To wit, that God was in Christ, reconciling the world unto himself, not imputing their trespasses unto them; and hath committed unto us the word of reconciliation. Now then we are ambassadors for Christ, as though God did beseech you by us: we pray you in Christ's stead, be ye reconciled to God." **2 CORINTHIANS 5:19–20**

Years ago, Anissa Ayala was diagnosed with leukemia. If she could not find a bone marrow transplant after radiation and chemotherapy, she would die.

Her parents desperately searched for a match, and when they could not find one, knew they needed to take drastic action. They decided to have another baby, hoping this child would be a match and save Anissa's life.

The baby, named Marissa, was an exact match.

As the story spread throughout the news, Marissa was hailed as someone who, quite literally, was born to save a life.[1]

Just as Marissa was born to rescue Anissa from her cancer, Jesus was born to rescue us from sin and offer complete forgiveness for all our wrongdoings. He desires nothing more than reconciliation, or "to be called back to union or friendship" with you! What an amazing, life-changing gift!

After we accept this gift of salvation, we then have a responsibility to share that message of reconciliation with others. God's incredible gift of forgiveness is too amazing for us to keep to ourselves.

1. "Woman Conceived More Than 2 Decades Ago To Save Sister's Life Graduates College," *CBS Los Angeles*, May 22, 2013, losangeles.cbslocal.com/2013/05/22/woman-conceived-in-1988-to-save-sisters-life-graduates-college/.

We have a life-changing gift that we can share with others who so desperately need it! As we have opportunities from God, may we share the gift of reconciliation and forgiveness with others.

REFLECT

What did God say to me as I read today's Scripture and devotion?

RESPOND

How does this apply to my life? What actions can I take because of what I've learned?

PRAY

"Lord, thank You for being born to save my life. Your gift of salvation is not something that I want to take for granted or keep to myself. I'm an ambassador for You with the privilege of sharing what You've done for me with a lost and dying world. Give me opportunities to share this message of love and forgiveness with others. Amen."

WEEK SIX | DAY THREE

ANGER BOMBS

"Let all bitterness, and wrath, and anger, and clamour, and evil speaking, be put away from you, with all malice." **EPHESIANS 4:31**

Steve Tran was frustrated with the cockroaches that constantly invaded his apartment. An article in the *Arizona Republic* records that he finally decided to purchase several bug bombs to assist in eradicating them. The problem was, he didn't use the bug bombs as the label indicated. Instead, he activated *twenty-five* of them, making the fumes reach the pilot light on his stove and causing a massive explosion with damages exceeding $10,000.[1]

Sometimes, we approach our relationships the way Steve Tran approached his cockroach problem. Instead of putting away ALL bitterness, anger, and wrath, we go about our day activating small anger bombs through the words we say, the looks we give, and the rejection we demonstrate. While these actions are intentional, we don't realize the true damage they bring to our relationships—and we later wonder why a conversation blew up or a friendship ended so abruptly.

If we want to get rid of the pesky irritations and issues we experience in our relationships, we have to start with eradicating issues of the heart first.

God instructs us in today's passage to put away bitterness, which is harboring unforgiveness. He asks us to remove wrath—fierce rage and passion— from our hearts.

1. "The Danger of Anger," *Ministry 127*, http://ministry127.com/resources/illustration/the-danger-of-anger, accessed April 28, 2019.

We are to put away anger, which is violent emotion, and clamor which involves loud complaining. (This carries the idea of someone taking to social media or some other public platform to complain.)

In addition, God tells us to put away evil speaking, such as slanders and lies that would destroy someone's reputation.

It's easy for any of us to "get out" these characteristics that God instructs us to "put away." So, let's be intentional in removing these habits and practicing forgiveness instead.

REFLECT

What did God say to me as I read today's Scripture and devotion?

RESPOND

How does this apply to my life? What actions can I take because of what I've learned?

PRAY

"Lord, sadly when I experience conflict in my relationships, I get out the very things You ask me to put away. Today, I confess my angry spirit and bitter heart to You. Please help me to put off wrath and evil speaking and put on edification, forgiveness, and kindness. Convict me when I'm falling into one of these forms of anger, and provoke me to instead please You in my interactions with others. Amen."

SEEKING REVENGE OR PURSUING PEACE

"Dearly beloved, avenge not yourselves, but rather give place unto wrath: for it is written, Vengeance is mine; I will repay, saith the Lord." **ROMANS 12:19**

When dealing with conflict, the opposite response of forgiveness is revenge. When someone wrongs us, the natural, fleshly response is often to get even. In some cases, we can even get so fixated on getting revenge that other areas of our lives begin to suffer.

God has called us to a better way. Instead of seeking revenge, He tells us to pursue forgiveness. Instead of harboring wrath, He commands us to seek peace.

Forgiveness is key to effective relationships. Why? It allows God to be in control of the outcome. As the ultimate Judge, He promises to repay in a way that is fitting and best. God's involvement is so much more effective than our own because His heart is pure. His perspective is eternal. And His love is constant for all involved.

Forgiveness not only gives God the opportunity to work, it also makes way for healing. When we choose to harbor bitterness, give place to wrath, or seek revenge, we hurt ourselves and others. But, when we let go of offenses and offer forgivness, we allow God to bring healing, freedom, and peace. May these characteristics define our lives as Christians seeking to honor the Lord, and may we commit the outcome of relational injustices to Him.

REFLECT

What did God say to me as I read today's Scripture and devotion?

RESPOND

How does this apply to my life? What actions can I take because of what I've learned?

PRAY

"Father, I come before You today, thanking You for being the righteous Judge You are. Thank You for the reminder that You are not only aware of relational conflict I experience, You are in control of making all things right. Today, I choose to rest in You—giving You what is rightfully Yours and surrendering the desire to get even when I am wronged. Help me to pursue peace, avoiding opportunities that would trigger an angry spirit. I rest in You today, and claim Your peace for my heart. In Your name I pray, Amen."

FORGIVE AS CHRIST FORGAVE

"And be ye kind one to another, tenderhearted, forgiving one another, even as God for Christ's sake hath forgiven you." **EPHESIANS 4:32**

Corrie ten Boom was a courageous Christian during the dark days of World War II. She hid Jews in her home from the Nazis, saving many lives. Finally, however, she and her family were caught and sent to Ravensbruck, a concentration camp of unspeakable atrocities. While she was there, her sister died.

Eventually, Corrie was released, and instead of growing bitter, she determined to encourage the hearts of thousands of others through her experiences. She journeyed throughout Europe, sharing her story.

In 1947, she stopped at a church in Munich and began speaking on forgiveness. After the service, a man walked up to Corrie. Immediately, she recognized him. He was one of the cruelest prison guards at Ravenbruck and had made her life miserable. As Corrie looked into his eyes, she didn't know how she could forgive him. She described her experience:

> Woodenly, mechanically, I thrust my hand into the one stretched out to me. And as I did, an incredible thing took place. The current started in my shoulder, raced down my arm, and sprang into our joined hands. And then this healing warmth seemed to flood my whole being, bringing tears to my eyes. "I forgive you, brother," I cried. "With all my heart!" For a long moment we grasped each other's hands, the former guard and the former prisoner. I had never known God's love so intensely as I did then.[1]

1. Corrie ten Boom, John Sherrill, and Elizabeth Sherrill, eds., *The Hiding Place* (Grand Rapids, MI: Chosen Books, 2006).

Forgiveness is never easy, but it is possible through Christ because of the forgiveness he offered to us. Do you need to extend the hand of forgiveness to someone today? May God grant you the strength to forgive as He forgave, and may you experience His richest blessings as you seek to honor Him in your relationships.

REFLECT

What did God say to me as I read today's Scripture and devotion?

RESPOND

How does this apply to my life? What actions can I take because of what I've learned?

PRAY

"Lord, I stand in awe of the incredible forgiveness that You extended to me on the cross. But I also admit that, at times, it can be so hard to forgive. So, please fill me with Your love and grace toward others. Help me to offer forgiveness and grace even when I don't feel like it. I claim Your strength to follow You on the path of obedience and restoration. In Jesus' name, Amen."

WHEREFORE COMFORT YOURSELVES TOGETHER, AND EDIFY ONE ANOTHER...

1 THESSALONIANS 5:11

WEEK SEVEN

COMFORT ONE ANOTHER

DAY 1: A Present Source of Comfort

DAY 2: Here on Earth Today, Home in Heaven Someday

DAY 3: Sober Living in Drunken Days

DAY 4: Alert: Attacks Ahead

DAY 5: Conduits of Comfort

7

COMFORT ONE ANOTHER

The afflictions and challenges of life can make us grow weary and despair. However, we who believe in Christ can take comfort that He is returning soon. In this study, we will learn how we can prepare for the Lord's return and comfort one another with the promise of eternity with God.

DISCUSSION

What are some of God's promises that have brought comfort to your heart during difficult times?

What are some characteristics that would define a Christian who is living in readiness for Christ's return?

What are the times in a believer's life when he or she may most need others to give comfort?

LESSON NOTES

WEEK SEVEN | DAY ONE

A PRESENT SOURCE OF COMFORT

"And I will pray the Father, and he shall give you another Comforter, that he may abide with you for ever; Even the Spirit of truth; whom the world cannot receive, because it seeth him not, neither knoweth him: but ye know him; for he dwelleth with you, and shall be in you." **JOHN 14:16–17**

What did you do for comfort the last time you faced a problem? Eat ice cream straight from the container? Pour out your sorrow to a friend? Turn to mindful meditation or pay top dollar for a professional counselor?

Too often, we seek external comfort for a quick fix to our emotional needs. We resort to our human wisdom to deal with problems. But as believers, we often fail to realize that the greatest source of comfort we have resides within us. It is exclusive to us as children of God, yet we fail to claim this privilege.

The Holy Spirit, who indwelt us at the moment of our salvation, is the Comforter sent by the Lord Jesus Christ to abide with us all through life. He knows our secret fears, our insecurities, our trials, our struggles, our relational dynamics—and He offers comfort through all of it. What a wonderful friend He is!

Those who do not know the Lord cannot experience the sweet comfort of His presence. But, as Christians, we have this wonderful reality and relationship!

Christ knew the grievances we would face in life and before we experienced them, He gave us the Comforter, ensuring we would have a friend and solution. We are not alone in our trials because the Holy Spirit abides with us, applying His healing balm to our sorrow and guiding us in the knowledge of God.

The Comforter is our safe refuge from the storms of life. Make Him your first resort and find in Him a lasting assurance.

REFLECT

What did God say to me as I read today's Scripture and devotion?

RESPOND

How does this apply to my life? What actions can I take because of what I've learned?

PRAY

"Lord, thank You for the gift of an abiding Comforter. When trials arise, remind me that I am not alone. I seek the comfort of Your Spirit who alone can bind my wounds, heal my heart, and make a way when there seems to be no way. I rest in You today, my dearest comforter and my greatest friend. Amen."

WEEK SEVEN | DAY TWO

HERE ON EARTH TODAY, HOME IN HEAVEN SOMEDAY

"We are confident, I say, and willing rather to be absent from the body, and to be present with the Lord. Wherefore we labour, that, whether present or absent, we may be accepted of him." **2 CORINTHIANS 5:8–9**

Ask the average person where he is headed to after this life and he would probably muse for a while, then mutter, "I don't know," or "Heaven, I hope." To the world, death is a dreaded event, an unwelcome passage to the great unknown.

The believer in Christ is not ignorant of his eternal destiny. He does not "hope" for Heaven when he dies. He knows he is Heaven bound. And his knowledge is founded on God's promise of eternity spent with Him. Because God's Word is sure, the believer can be confident that absence from the body is presence with the Lord forever. To the child of God, death is only a bridge to eternal glory.

So, how does this promise of heaven influence our everyday living? The knowledge that we will one day spend eternity with our God motivates us to please Him in all that we do. Whether in life or in death, our ambition is the Lord's approval.

The promise of Heaven fuels us with courage and tenacity to surmount every setback because victory is already ours in life and death. In life, we endeavor to live for His glory. In death, we enjoy a glorious eternity with Him.

What confidence we can have in Him! What comfort He gives! What assurance we possess. May we live with conviction today—motivated by our hearts for Him and by the wonderful reality that we will spend eternity with Him forever.

REFLECT

What did God say to me as I read today's Scripture and devotion?

RESPOND

How does this apply to my life? What actions can I take because of what I've learned?

PRAY

"Lord, in the busyness of life and realities of every day hardships, I can easily lose confidence. But in You, I find the comforting assurance that You are always with me—in life and in death. Thank You for the promise of eternal life in Your presence. Keep my eyes fixed on You and this blessed hope of Heaven as I sojourn through life, seeking to please You in everything I do. Thank You for the confidence I have in You alone. Amen."

SOBER LIVING IN DRUNKEN DAYS

"Awake to righteousness, and sin not; for some have not the knowledge of God: I speak this to your shame." **1 CORINTHIANS 15:34**

During the Gulf War in 1990 when Iraq invaded Kuwait, British Prime Minister Margaret Thatcher gave this advice to President George H. W. Bush: "Remember, George, this is no time to go wobbly."

Her stiff charge became a memorable catchphrase that captured the attention of both politicians and the masses.

The apostle Paul's warning to the Corinthians against the corruption of false doctrine echoes the Iron Lady's injunction. At the time of his writing, the Corinthians had been swayed by the false teaching that denied the bodily resurrection of Christ after His death on the cross. Paul urged the Corinthian believers to awake to truth from their intoxication of falsehood.

The doctrinal errors of Paul's time may not apply to us now, but the call to spiritual sobriety still rings true today.

Heresies of different sorts continue to abound, contaminating the truth of God's Word. Movements abound today that promote "feel-goodism" and religious tolerance at the expense of absolute truth. It is a shame that we who have the truth should be led astray by those who have no knowledge of God.

Perilous times call for prudent living.

Let us walk in righteousness according to the light of God's Word. Let us be serious about the things of God, and then comfort one another with the truth of hope that is found in Jesus.

REFLECT

What did God say to me as I read today's Scripture and devotion?

RESPOND

How does this apply to my life? What actions can I take because of what I've learned?

PRAY

"Lord, keep me vigilant in this day of evil falsehood. Protect my heart from teaching or beliefs that would lead me away from You. Give me a sober mind and a tender heart to Your truth. Let my life be a beacon of truth that guides others to the knowledge of You. Instruct me in sober, holy living that I might be found worthy of my calling. Amen."

ALERT: ATTACKS AHEAD

"Stand therefore, having your loins girt about with truth, and having on the breastplate of righteousness; and take the helmet of salvation, and the sword of the Spirit, which is the word of God:" **EPHESIANS 6:14, 17**

The Christian life is no walk in the park. While we are given victory over sin through Jesus Christ, we still face challenges each day that require faith, courage, and determination. These challenges will overwhelm us if we are not prepared to deal with them.

The Bible likens the Christian life to a battleground. It is an intense spiritual warfare against a relentless enemy—the devil—"a roaring lion...seeking whom he may devour" (1 Peter 5:8). Satan knows he cannot rob us of our salvation, and is thus on the prowl each day, waiting to pounce on us unaware and hinder our progress in the faith.

We cannot fight this battle with the devil on our own. To win it, we need to be fully equipped with the full armor of God. Our first step to success in this battle is adopting the right stance.

We are to stand in, or to hold on to a position of readiness. No soldier enters a battle sitting or slouching, but firmly planted on his two feet, ready to launch forward.

The Christian soldier's attire is also fit for battle. He puts on the belt of truth—which supports the rest of his armor. Without the brace of God's truth, he is left vulnerable to the blows of false teaching. He also dons the breastplate of righteousness, which involves obeying God's commandments and living honorably.

The helmet of salvation protects the Christian soldier's head with the assurance of his salvation. It gives him the certainty that he is fighting from victory and that his eternity is secured in Heaven. Finally, the Christian soldier takes up the sword of the Spirit, or the Word of God. To use this weapon skillfully, he must study the Scriptures and thoroughly understand its truths. With the full armor on, the Christian soldier will triumph over every attack and emerge victorious in every battle.

As believers, we are to be prepared for the return of the Lord—spiritually alert and ready to stand against Satan's attacks. Put on your armor. Stand firm, and claim the victory that is yours in Jesus Christ.

REFLECT

What did God say to me as I read today's Scripture and devotion?

RESPOND

How does this apply to my life? What actions can I take because of what I've learned?

PRAY

"Lord, I realize that the Christian life is a spiritual battle. Help me put on the full armor of God and empower me to conquer the foe daily. Thank You for promising me the victory. Give me the strength to fight the good fight of faith to the very end. Amen."

CONDUITS OF COMFORT

"Blessed be God, even the Father of our Lord Jesus Christ, the Father of mercies, and the God of all comfort; Who comforteth us in all our tribulation, that we may be able to comfort them which are in any trouble, by the comfort wherewith we ourselves are comforted of God." **2 CORINTHIANS 1:3–4**

Given a choice, we'd choose comfort over discomfort anytime. We want to coast through life without surviving the storms or braving the bumps and bruises. The comfortable life is the coveted life—but is ultimately an unprofitable life. It does nothing to mature us in the faith, move us to seek divine comfort, or make us sensitive to the suffering of others.

The apostle Paul was able to praise God for His mercies and comfort because of the years spent in the school of suffering. He was a man well-acquainted with affliction. And in each affliction, He found that God's divine consolation exceeded the sorrow of his suffering. Having personally experienced the blessing of God's strength in his weakness, he then exhorts us to embrace trials so we may be recipients of divine compassion and channel His comfort to others who are hurting.

Trials are a gift, not a grievance. Beneath the uncomely packaging of trials lies the goodness of God's comfort.

Are you going through a trial today? Rest in the truth that you are in the best place to experience His comfort. And with that comfort comes the benefit of sharing His comfort with others. May we be conduits of His comfort, channels of His grace, ministers of His goodness.

REFLECT

What did God say to me as I read today's Scripture and devotion?

RESPOND

How does this apply to my life? What actions can I take because of what I've learned?

PRAY

"Lord, I'm experiencing a season of discomfort that is challenging me in ways I didn't know it would. Help me see the good You bring out of every bad thing. Take my hurt and heal it with Your comfort. Help me to rest in Your mercy, and then use me to minister this comfort to others who are hurting, too. Amen."

LET US THEREFORE FOLLOW AFTER THE THINGS WHICH MAKE FOR PEACE, AND THINGS WHEREWITH ONE MAY EDIFY ANOTHER.

ROMANS 14:19

WEEK EIGHT

EDIFY ONE ANOTHER

DAY 1: Edify to Unify

DAY 2: Surrender Is Sweet

DAY 3: The Gift of Grace

DAY 4: Forwarding Faith

DAY 5: Mind Your Mouth

8

EDIFY ONE ANOTHER

God wants us to pursue peace in our relationships with one another to preserve the unity of the church. In this study, we learn how we can live peaceably with one another and how we can avoid causing others to stumble. Through edification, we can help others grow in spiritual maturity.

DISCUSSION

Who in your life can you purposely seek to build up this week?

Who has God put in your life to help build you up in spiritual maturity?

What ministry in your church are you involved in (or would you like to be involved in)? Who could you reach out to, encouraging others to join you in the work of the ministry?

LESSON NOTES

WEEK EIGHT | DAY ONE

EDIFY TO UNIFY

"For the kingdom of God is not meat and drink; but righteousness, and peace, and joy in the Holy Ghost. For he that in these things serveth Christ is acceptable to God, and approved of men. Let us therefore follow after the things which make for peace, and things wherewith one may edify another."
ROMANS 14:17–19

When we receive Christ, we are born into His family and enter into a relationship not just with Him, but with our brothers and sisters in Christ. We might have our different practices or preferences, but the gel that holds us together is our common faith in God.

However, if we aren't careful, we can tear the fabric of unity when we exert our rights to liberty. Instead of stirring contention over petty issues or causing a brother to stumble because of our actions, we are to simply serve the Lord in righteousness, peace, and joy. When we do so, God is pleased with our way of life, and men will commend our godly conduct.

As members of the body of Christ, let us lay aside strife and contention and pursue the spirit of peace. Speak words of encouragement to a friend who is facing a crisis. Thank your Bible study leader for preparing the lesson. Pay a visit to a family who hasn't been coming to church. Bear the burdens of your pastor by praying for him.

When we build up one another through acts of love, we strengthen our bonds in Christ and reflect the love of God to an unloving world.

Who can you edify today? How can you follow after things that make for peace? Step forward and encourage those God has put in your path this week.

REFLECT

What did God say to me as I read today's Scripture and devotion?

RESPOND

How does this apply to my life? What actions can I take because of what I've learned?

PRAY

"Lord, help me to seek the interests of others above mine. May my manner of life be pleasing before You and lead others to praise You. Show me how I can be an encouragement to someone in need of it today. Amen."

WEEK EIGHT | DAY TWO

SURRENDER IS SWEET

"For none of us liveth to himself, and no man dieth to himself. For whether we live, we live unto the Lord; and whether we die, we die unto the Lord: whether we live therefore, or die, we are the Lord's." **ROMANS 14:7–8**

The world says, "You only live once—live for yourself." The Lord says, "Only one life to live, live it for my glory."

The Christian life is the crucified life. We are no longer our own because God has purchased us with His redeeming blood. He paid the price we could not pay. And we are now His property in life and death.

We live for no other purpose than His. We know no other will than His. We serve no other Master than Him. We seek no other approval but His.

When you examine your present life, can you say with certainty that you're living for Christ? Is all your effort and hard work for personal recognition? Is your display of talent for men's praise? Are you living for yourself?

Living for the Lord begins with dying to self, denying selfish and sinful pleasures. That may sound severe—but surrender is actually a blessing, not a burden! The crucified life gives us more than we lose. When we surrender to live for the Lord, we find that our heavenly gains far exceed our earthly losses.

The life we live in Him requires sacrifice, but it brings lasting satisfaction.

So, ~~we~~ have two choices: One is to serve self. The other is to serve the Saviour. One will give you pleasure for a season. The other will give you pleasure for eternity. What will you chose today?

REFLECT

What did God say to me as I read today's Scripture and devotion?

RESPOND

How does this apply to my life? What actions can I take because of what I've learned?

PRAY

"Lord, because You've redeemed me with Your precious blood, I am Your possession. I yield my life as an offering to You. Use it to bring You glory; You are worthy of it all. Thank You for the assurance that what I do for You will last for eternity. Help me to pursue Your glory, Your pleasure, Your fame in this life you've given me. I want to live for You alone. Amen."

THE GIFT OF GRACE

"For the grace of God that bringeth salvation hath appeared to all men, Teaching us that, denying ungodliness and worldly lusts, we should live soberly, righteously, and godly, in this present world." **TITUS 2:11–12**

We often hear the word grace. But what does it really mean and what does it do in our lives?

Grace is God's unmerited favor. It is getting what we do not deserve. We deserve eternal death for our sins, but God's grace brought us salvation. And this salvation is for all men. No one is too sinful to receive forgiveness. No sin is too great for grace to overcome. God's grace leads us to salvation because it reveals His unconditional love for us.

But God's grace doesn't just stop at salvation. His undeserved favor toward us continues its work by transforming our lives. His grace enables us to live for Him. It brings about a forsaking of sin and a following after Christ.

When we have experienced the goodness of God's grace in saving us, we then will want to please Him by obeying His commandments and denying ungodliness and worldly lusts. The things of God become more important than the things of the world. This was evident in the apostle Paul's life. His conversion brought a paradigm shift—he counted the loss of all things that he might win Christ (Philippians 3:8). "All things" included the worldly privileges, carnal pleasures, and the comforts of life.

God's grace at work in our lives through power of the Holy Spirit enables us to produce the fruit of righteousness. It motivates us to live soberly in a world of riotous living. It cultivates in us a healthy fear of the Lord that drives us to lead godly lives.

Though we may stumble or fail, God's grace in the finished work of the cross allows us to get back up and continue striving to please Him. We seek to live righteously not because it saves us, but because His amazing, saving grace compels us.

REFLECT

What did God say to me as I read today's Scripture and devotion?

RESPOND

How does this apply to my life? What actions can I take because of what I've learned?

PRAY

"Lord, thank You for saving me by grace through faith. Thank You for supplying abundant grace to live the Christian life. Please help me as I seek to live soberly, righteously, and godly in this present world. Let Your loving favor empower me for the challenges each day brings and draw me yet closer to You. Amen."

FORWARDING FAITH

"Night and day praying exceedingly that we might see your face, and might perfect that which is lacking in your faith? And the Lord make you to increase and abound in love one toward another, and toward all men, even as we do toward you." **1 THESSALONIANS 3:10, 12**

Your spiritual growth is the result of someone's investment in you. Perhaps your parent planted the seed of salvation during your childhood. Your Sunday school teacher nurtured that seed into a seedling through the watering of God's Word. Your pastor then matured that seedling into a fruit-bearing tree with the fertilizer of sound doctrine. Aren't you thankful that someone cared to help you grow in your faith?

The apostle Paul was a spiritual father with deep interest in the welfare of his children in the faith. His ministry to the young believers in Thessalonica had ended abruptly with his departure to avoid imprisonment. Concerned for the well-being of the newborn church, he prayed earnestly to meet them again and establish them in the faith. He wanted the Thessalonian Christians to be grounded in the Word of God that they might remain steadfast amid persecution. He also desired their love for one another to grow not only within the church family but also toward all men. Charity is one of the defining qualities of the Christian faith. By abounding in love for each other and everyone else, the young believers would demonstrate the perfecting of their faith.

God has used mature Christians to help us develop spiritually, and He wants us to continue this good work by investing in other believers. As we have been nurtured in God's truth, so let us also build others up in the faith. May our love increase and abound toward one another and all men as we continue on the path of spiritual maturity and edification.

REFLECT

What did God say to me as I read today's Scripture and devotion?

RESPOND

How does this apply to my life? What actions can I take because of what I've learned?

PRAY

"Lord, thank You for those who have gone before me on my journey of spiritual growth. Thank You for the investment that was made and for the nurturing that took place, bringing me to this point. As I mature in my walk with You, teach me to invest in the spiritual growth of others as well. May my love and investment increase toward those You've placed in my life. Please use me to make a difference in the lives of others. Amen."

WEEK EIGHT | DAY FIVE

MIND YOUR MOUTH

"Let no corrupt communication proceed out of your mouth, but that which is good to the use of edifying, that it may minister grace unto the hearers."
EPHESIANS 4:29

What's in a word? The power to build or destroy, bless or blame, heal or kill.

Of the thousands of words we speak each day, how many of them are used to minister grace? How many of these words could be described as corrupt communication?

Because our words have such a great impact on others, we are reminded to guard what comes out of our mouths. We cannot *reverse* what we *converse*. Often, the damage caused by a verbal attack exceeds the repair of our apology. On the contrary, God says our words should be sweet to the hearer—edifying and gracious. Your interactions with others are opportunities to season your words with encouragement, kindness, and grace.

The world has enough corrupt communication. Are you adding to it or countering it with words that nourish?

During His earthly ministry, the Lord Jesus Christ spoke life-giving words that healed the broken, raised the dead, and strengthened the weak. It should be our desire to emulate Him and minister to others with our words.

You have the power today to soothe or sting someone with your speech. Identify ways to edify a colleague, church friend, sibling, or stranger. Use your words as a ministry to encourage. Share a praise, show your appreciation, say something pleasant to someone who has had a rough day. Proverbs 15:23 says: "A man hath joy by the answer of his mouth: and a word spoken in due season, how good is it!"

May God use us to speak gracious and edifying words to others this week!

REFLECT

What did God say to me as I read today's Scripture and devotion?

RESPOND

How does this apply to my life? What actions can I take because of what I've learned?

PRAY

"Lord, set a watch over my lips. Give me wisdom with my words, that they may communicate grace, truth, and love to those around me. Please speak through me, that I may be a blessing, rather than a burden to others. Help me to follow Your example as I minister to others through kind and Christ-honoring speech. Amen."

FINALLY, BE YE ALL OF ONE MIND, HAVING COMPASSION ONE OF ANOTHER...

1 PETER 3:8

WEEK NINE

COMPASSION FOR ONE ANOTHER

DAY 1: The Good of Gratitude

DAY 2: Comfort Zones and Compassion

DAY 3: The Counter-Culture Christian

DAY 4: No One Like Him

DAY 5: The Best Is Yet to Come

9

COMPASSION FOR ONE ANOTHER

God has called all of us to extend His compassion for us to one another. But demonstrating compassion in our busy, daily lives is often easier said than done, especially in the selfish and indifferent society in which we live. In this study, we look at how we can purposefully make a difference in the lives of others by showing compassion through our words and deeds.

DISCUSSION

What are five blessings God has given you for which you can give thanks?

What are tangible, practical ways to demonstrate compassion to those in need?

It's always easier to feel compassion toward those who are kind to us. How can we increase our compassion for those who are unkind to us?

LESSON NOTES

WEEK NINE | DAY ONE

THE GOOD OF GRATITUDE

"Enter into his gates with thanksgiving, and into his courts with praise: be thankful unto him, and bless his name. For the LORD is good; his mercy is everlasting; and his truth endureth to all generations." **PSALM 100:4–5**

William Arthur Ward said, "Feeling gratitude and not expressing it is like wrapping a present and not giving it." Gratitude and the act of giving go hand in hand. True thankfulness extends beyond the realm of feeling grateful and galvanizes the person to acts of compassion.

When you've experienced the joy of *receiving* a blessing, you want to share that joy by *giving* others a blessing. Perhaps you've once received the gift of money during a time of financial need. This sum of money helped to pay your bills and brought great relief in your desperation. Years later, you learn of someone else who is struggling to make ends meet. You not only empathize with his plight but are motivated to give. Why? Your gratitude for your previous blessing compelled you to express compassion in action.

Have you wondered why the Bible constantly exhorts us to give thanks? Sometimes, it almost seems like a given. The truth is, gratitude is good for us because of what it does in us. It not only motivates us to show compassion, it also keeps us from covetousness. When we count our blessings, we realize how much God has given us and learn to find joy in contentment.

Thankfulness also teaches us to look to God and not on our circumstances. Our situation may not change for the better, but we can be thankful for a God who never changes. As you begin this week, consider starting a journal to record all of God's answers to your prayers. As you reflect on how He has provided for your needs over the years, you will be reminded that He is a God who never fails.

Gratitude—it is good for us! It lends toward compassion. It keeps our focus on the Giver of our blessings, and it helps us cultivate contentment. May we begin this week with hearts of gratitude for the blessings given to us by God.

REFLECT

What did God say to me as I read today's Scripture and devotion?

RESPOND

How does this apply to my life? What actions can I take because of what I've learned?

PRAY

"Lord, as I focus my heart on the virtue of compassion this week, I pause now to simply thank You for Your compassion toward me. Thank You for the blessings You've bestowed in my life. You've given me more than I deserve—including the incredible gift of salvation. Give me an attitude of gratitude that acknowledges You in everything I receive. May all my days be filled with praise expressed to You for who You are and what You've done. Then, may I express compassion to others in need. Amen."

COMFORT ZONES AND COMPASSION

"And Jesus went forth, and saw a great multitude, and was moved with compassion toward them, and he healed their sick." **MATTHEW 14:14**

When the realist sees the multitude, he sees problems. When the idealist sees the multitude, he sees opportunity.

When you see the multitude, what do you see? Hypocrisy, busyness, or hostility, perhaps?

The busyness of life has, to some extent, made us indifferent to the people around us. Everyday, we weave through traffic, move through the mob, and stare at our phones as we march to our destinations, without pausing to consider the people we pass by. These are people we may even cross paths with often, yet to us, they remain nameless faces among the masses. We mind our own business, not caring to spare a thought for the person next to us.

Notice in Matthew 14:14 that Jesus *went forth*. He stepped out from his place of rest, perhaps a ship or a desert, where He sought refuge from the swelling crowd. He had His time of retreat, and now it was time to advance. And when He saw the multitude, He was moved with compassion. He saw people with needs—both physical and spiritual. They were afflicted with bodily ailments and "were as sheep not having a shepherd" (Mark 6:34). Stirred with sympathy, the tender Saviour acted on their needs—He healed their sick and fed their souls the words of God.

Through Christ's response to the multitude, we learn to step out of our own comfort zones and see people as individuals with spiritual and physical needs. Our primary concern for others should be that they have a relationship with the Lord. But,

Jesus did not only care for the welfare of lost souls. He also ministered to physical needs. Do you know someone in need today? Has God laid a person on your heart who would benefit from your compassion and concern for them? Proverbs 3:27 instructs us not to withhold our help to our neighbor when it is in our power to provide assistance.

Cotton Mather, a Puritan preacher, once said, "The opportunity to do good imposes the obligation to do it." Today, may we be compelled by our love for Christ to fulfill the holy obligation of doing good to others. Let's step out of our comfort zones to show compassion to those in need.

REFLECT

What did God say to me as I read today's Scripture and devotion?

RESPOND

How does this apply to my life? What actions can I take because of what I've learned?

PRAY

"Lord, forgive me for my indifference to people. In the busyness of my life, I often neglect to notice the needs of those around me. Help me see the multitude through the lens of Your love. Help me to see my family through the lens of Your love. May I minister to those at church and work who You've laid on my heart. Let Your compassion flow through me and move me to minister to the needs of others. Amen."

THE COUNTER-CULTURE CHRISTIAN

"But I say unto you, Love your enemies, bless them that curse you, do good to them that hate you, and pray for them which despitefully use you, and persecute you." **MATTHEW 5:44**

Christian conduct runs counter to the culture of the world. Society tells you to hate your enemies, curse them that curse you, do evil to them that hate you, and provoke them which despitefully use you and persecute you.

Scriptures tell you the complete opposite. What do you do to your enemies? Love them. To those who curse you? Bless them. To those who hate you? Do good to them. To those who despitefully use and persecute you? Pray for them. Sounds like a tall order. Can you actually do all that? The answer is no, not on your own.

Returning evil with good is only possible through Christ who strengthens you (Philippians 4:13). He loved you when you were unlovable. He cared for you when you didn't care for Him. He saved you when you were steeped in sin. His love will compel you and His Spirit enable you to show compassion in the face of conflict.

If we are to have an effective testimony to unbelievers, our lifestyles need to be distinguished from theirs. First Peter 2:9 refers to the children of God as "a peculiar people." A Christian's manner of life should strike the world as uniquely identified with Christ.

Does your language blend with the world's? Does your anger match theirs when conflict arises? Do you get even when offended? The difference in your life should be so attractive and refreshing that others want that difference in their lives too.

REFLECT

What did God say to me as I read today's Scripture and devotion?

RESPOND

How does this apply to my life? What actions can I take because of what I've learned?

PRAY

"Lord, let Your light shine in this world of darkness through my words, deeds, and conduct. Help me make a difference in the lives of others by having a testimony that is distinct from the world and a heart that is compassionate toward all people—even my enemies. I thank You for the power You give me to accomplish this even in seemingly impossible situations. Please give me the wisdom I need to navigate difficult relationships. Thank You for the grace and power You bestow to enable me to have a testimony that is pleasing to You. Amen."

WEEK NINE | DAY FOUR

NO ONE LIKE HIM

"Who is a God like unto thee, that pardoneth iniquity, and passeth by the transgression of the remnant of his heritage? he retaineth not his anger for ever, because he delighteth in mercy. He will turn again, he will have compassion upon us; he will subdue our iniquities; and thou wilt cast all their sins into the depths of the sea." **MICAH 7:18–19**

Vast, mighty, overwhelming, and unfathomable—the ocean is filled with endless wonder. The same can be said of God's mercy and compassion, which know no boundaries.

Our sin might be great but His mercy is greater. Our sin might incur His wrath, but His mercy outweighs His anger. His compassion sweeps over us in forgiveness, casting our sins into the depths of the sea and remembering them no more. Like the rise and fall of the ocean, this cycle of God's mercy and compassion are constant. And this steadfastness of His goodness supplies us with the strength each day to row our boats against the currents of life.

Lamentations 3:22–23 speaks of the daily mercy and compassion God gives: "It is of the Lord's mercies that we are not consumed, because his compassions fail not. They are new every morning: great is thy faithfulness."

God's mercy and compassion are just two of His many amazing attributes! When you begin to consider them and what they mean to you, you have only just scratched the surface. It will take eternity to discover who God is, but it isn't too early to experience His lovingkindness and compassion.

Have you paused recently to truly consider who God is? As you seek to show compassion, have you contemplated the unparalleled compassion of God?

Pull away from the distractions of life. Get off the grid for a time, and be still. Get to know the God who delights in showing mercy. As you ponder His divine attributes, you will find yourself lost in wonder, and like the prophet Micah, your lips will praise Him: "Who is a God like unto thee?"

REFLECT

What did God say to me as I read today's Scripture and devotion?

RESPOND

How does this apply to my life? What actions can I take because of what I've learned?

PRAY

"Lord, thank You for your boundless mercy and compassion. Help me see Your goodness at work in my everyday life and rejoice in it. Fill my days with endless wonder in knowing You, a God unlike any other. Amen."

WEEK NINE | DAY FIVE

THE BEST IS YET TO COME

"And let us not be weary in well doing: for in due season we shall reap, if we faint not." **GALATIANS 6:9**

Laboring for the Lord is exciting. We get to invest in eternity and serve an almighty God. But as time progresses, the excitement can wear off and give way to exhaustion and even discouragement. Perhaps you've spent months discipling a new convert who still does not attend church regularly. Perhaps you've been trying to witness to your colleagues but keep facing rejection and ridicule. Maybe you've tried to show compassion and love to someone who refuses to accept your gestures of kindness. It's easy to contemplate quitting when you don't see the results for which you hoped. *Is the investment worth it? Am I truly making a difference?*

You are not alone in your struggle. Even the great prophet Elijah was not immune to fatigue and despair. In fact, his moment of discouragement came hot on the heels of a great victory. He had just demonstrated God's power by calling down fire from Heaven and later, sending a rainstorm after a three-year drought. Yet when he learned of Jezebel's order to kill him, he fled to the wilderness and requested God to take away his life. He had grown weary in serving the Lord.

What will keep us going when the going gets tough? The promise of a reward. We will reap in due season if we faint not. The hard work in the fields will bring a harvest. But it will be realized only after a period of perseverance and at God's appointed time. The wait may be long, the work may be wearying, the outcome may be different than planned—but the reaping will be worth it.

Christ, our greatest example of compassion, endured the cross, because He knew the result would be salvation for mankind. With that in mind, He found the strength to bear the weight of the world's sins and the suffering.

What is the cross you're bearing today? What relational struggle weighs you down as you pray for a positive outcome? Bear it patiently, and keep your eyes on the Lord, who is our ultimate reward. The best is yet to come. First Corinthians 2:9 says: "But as it is written, Eye hath not seen, nor ear heard, neither have entered into the heart of man, the things which God hath prepared for them that love him."

REFLECT

What did God say to me as I read today's Scripture and devotion?

RESPOND

How does this apply to my life? What actions can I take because of what I've learned?

PRAY

"Lord, thank You for enduring the cross to save me. Thank You for pressing forward in the face of conflict. Please empower me to continue investing in my relationships, following Your example of perseverance. Please give me the strength to persevere in well-doing. Help me finish this race strong, trusting You for the results and claiming Your promise of fruit in due season. Amen."

AND ABOVE
ALL THINGS
HAVE FERVENT
CHARITY AMONG
YOURSELVES...

1 PETER 4:8

WEEK TEN

MINISTER TO ONE ANOTHER

DAY 1: My Goal: God's Glory

DAY 2: Love Covers

DAY 3: Love Speaks in Deeds

DAY 4: To Abide Is to Abound

DAY 5: The Least Is the Greatest

10

MINISTER TO ONE ANOTHER

Not every Christian works in full-time church ministry, but every Christian is called to full-time Christianity. And this includes ministering to one another. God wants us to serve one another in love and show hospitality by opening our hearts and homes to others. He has also endowed us with spiritual gifts that He wants us to use in ministering to one another.

DISCUSSION

Sometimes we go to church looking for what we can get out of it. What are ways in which we can look for opportunities to show love to others at church?

What are some of the best ways to show hospitality to others? What are some tips you have discovered to make showing hospitality more doable?

What have you found that helps bring spiritual renewal when you grow exhausted through service to others?

LESSON NOTES

WEEK TEN | DAY ONE

MY GOAL: GOD'S GLORY

"If any man speak, let him speak as the oracles of God; if any man minister, let him do it as of the ability which God giveth: that God in all things may be glorified through Jesus Christ, to whom be praise and dominion for ever and ever. Amen." **1 PETER 4: 11**

The Word of God is one of God's greatest gifts to us. It shows us the way to salvation, it instructs us in the way of godly living, it comforts us when we are weary, it reproves us when we err, and it discerns our thoughts and motives.

We are to believe, study, obey—but also, we are to proclaim—the Word. When we speak, our words should accurately reflect the truth of God's Word. If any man speak, let him speak according to the words of God.

As we share God's Word with others, we can do so compassionately and kindly, but also with boldness and conviction, because truly, His Word has the power to purify and change us (John 17:17).

Just as our words are to communicate God's truth, our service ought to be carried out in God's strength. Every saint is called to serve God, and with this calling comes the enablement of God. The burdens of ministering can be overwhelming at times, and if we rely on our own strength, we will fall under the load. However, when we rely on God's strength to do His Work, we can continue steadfastly.

Would your speech and service to others align with the description given in 1 Peter 4:11? Have you been sharing God's truth or your opinions? Has your service been enabled by Him or has it been done in your own strength? Have you glorified God in your interactions with others?

The end goal of our communication and ministering is to bring glory to God. He has given us the gift of His Word and His strength, and in return, we give Him praise and honor as we seek to live in a way that pleases Him in our speech and service.

REFLECT

What did God say to me as I read today's Scripture and devotion?

RESPOND

How does this apply to my life? What actions can I take because of what I've learned?

PRAY

"Lord, use my lips to speak Your truth and my hands to do Your work. Let all that I say and do bring You glory for all that I have comes from You. Thank You for creating me to bring You glory. Please help me to live my life to that end as I seek to fulfill Your purposes and find my fulfillment in You alone. Amen."

LOVE COVERS

"Hatred stirreth up strifes: but love covereth all sins." **PROVERBS 10:12**

Picture a small, crackling bonfire. Now, imagine what would happen if someone took handfuls of dry wood and leaves, doused them with gasoline, and tossed them at the fire. The fire would immediately grow. In contrast, imagine what would happen if someone threw sand on the fire. The sand would smother the fire, extinguishing the flames. This idea of sand and gasoline pictures love and hate. Hate adds fuel to the fire of strife. It agitates and instigates conflict. But, just as sand extinguishes a fire, love smooths and sweeps over all sins and covers them in forgiveness. Hate reveals the faults of others and divides people, but love conceals offences and restores relations. Hate is a troublemaker; love is a peacemaker.

Malice has no place in the Christian life. The world is rife with gossip, slander, backbiting, and envying because it does not know God. Love, however, is one of the hallmarks of the Christian because it reflects the character of God. We are called to "...love one another: for love is of God; and every one that loveth is born of God, and knoweth God" (1 John 4:7). Our love for one another will show the world that we are Christ's disciples (John 13:35).

Loving others begins with loving God. He has demonstrated the greatest love by giving His Son to die for us. Isaiah 43:25 tells us that He has blotted out our transgressions and remembers them no more. If God has wiped our slate clean, we have no reason to bear a grudge against a brother. God's love toward us will constrain us to forgive others the way He forgives us; His love will spur us to love others the way He loves us. When we channel His love to others, we draw them back to the source of all love—God Himself.

As we seek to serve others, may we do so in love. May we demonstrate a positive, passionate love. A love that is from God. A love that shows up. A love that forgives trespasses. A love that gives grace.

REFLECT

What did God say to me as I read today's Scripture and devotion?

RESPOND

How does this apply to my life? What actions can I take because of what I've learned?

PRAY

"Lord, I confess to You that there have been times in my life when I've stirred up strife rather than covered situations in love. Thank You for showing me what love is. Help me be an agent of Your love to others, even those who are most difficult to love. I pray that my life will be a beautiful masterpiece that smooths and covers offenses in forgiveness and grace. Amen."

WEEK TEN | DAY THREE

LOVE SPEAKS IN DEEDS

"Distributing to the necessity of saints; given to hospitality." **ROMANS 12:13**

True love manifests itself in action. Your verbal expression of "I love you" will not mean anything until you demonstrate that love. God demonstrated His love for us by sending His Son to die on the cross. The father of the prodigal son demonstrated his love by preparing an elaborate feast to welcome him back. Mary demonstrated her love for the Lord by anointing His feet with an alabaster jar of ointment. The good Samaritan demonstrated his love to the injured man by treating his wounds and providing him lodging. We demonstrate our love for the Lord by doing what He has commanded in meeting the needs of our brothers and sisters in Christ.

First John 3:18 tells us not to "...love in word, neither in tongue; but in deed and in truth." One way in which we put love into action is by ministering to the needs of our fellow Christians. These needs include caring for the sick, cheering the depressed, counseling the struggling, and comforting the sorrowful.

We are also to show our love by sharing God's blessings. We give to others as God has given us, and to whom much is given, much is required (Luke 12:48). If God has blessed us materially, we ought to give generously to those in financial need. As we give, we find that God gives us more, not necessarily in monetary terms, but in the things that money cannot buy—joy, peace, and contentment.

Giving to others goes beyond gifts of monetary value. Most of us have a roof over our heads and that itself is an opportunity to extend hospitality to others. What does it mean to be given to hospitality? The word given in Romans 12:13 translates from the Greek word that means "to aggressively pursue." We are to welcome guests to our homes the way God welcomes us to His presence. He invites us and receives us as we are. Hospitality is not only about opening our homes, but our hearts, too. It is welcoming people to a safe space where they find comfort, compassion, and encouragement.

In 2 Timothy 1:16–17, the Apostle Paul gives special mention to Onesiphorus for his hospitality: "The Lord give mercy unto the house of Onesiphorus; for he oft refreshed me, and was not ashamed of my chain: But, when he was in Rome, he sought me out very diligently, and found me." May it be our prayer that we passionately pursue generosity and hospitality in our God-given relationships.

REFLECT

What did God say to me as I read today's Scripture and devotion?

RESPOND

How does this apply to my life? What actions can I take because of what I've learned?

PRAY

"Lord, help me see the needs of others as an opportunity to demonstrate Your love. Open my heart and my home to minister to others and refresh their souls. Thank You for giving to me and for inviting me into Your presence. May I do the same for others this week, I pray. Amen."

WEEK TEN | DAY FOUR

TO ABIDE IS TO ABOUND

"Abide in me, and I in you. As the branch cannot bear fruit of itself, except it abide in the vine; no more can ye, except ye abide in me. I am the vine, ye are the branches: He that abideth in me, and I in him, the same bringeth forth much fruit: for without me ye can do nothing." **JOHN 15:4–5**

Grapes grow on branches that in turn, grow on the vine. If we are to bear fruit of the Spirit, we need to be attached to Christ and depend on Him for growth to take place. Christ likens Himself to a grape vine, and us to branches. He is the source of our nourishment and feeds us with life-giving nutrients that enable us to flourish and bear fruit. Just as the branches draw water and nutrients from the vine, so we need to draw our strength and sustenance from Christ.

Abiding in Christ is a state of complete dependence. Trying to do good deeds in your own strength is like a branch trying to grow fruit on its own—it will not work. The branch needs to be attached to the vine to fulfill its function of bearing fruit. To abound in service and ministry to others, we need to be abiding in the Word of God, walking in the Spirit, and letting God have total mastery over our lives.

When we bear fruit, we manifest the work of Christ in our lives. Our reliance on Him to produce fruit prompts humility because we acknowledge that apart from God, we can do nothing. The fruit we bear is the sole result of God working in us. And because of that God receives all the glory.

REFLECT

What did God say to me as I read today's Scripture and devotion?

RESPOND

How does this apply to my life? What actions can I take because of what I've learned?

PRAY

"Lord, forgive me for trying to function and serve in my own effort. My works are futile without Your partnership. Quench my thirst with Your living water and feed me the Bread of Life that I may receive nourishment to bear fruit for You. Amen."

THE LEAST IS THE GREATEST

"...but whosoever will be great among you, shall be your minister: And whosoever of you will be the chiefest, shall be servant of all. For even the Son of man came not to be ministered unto, but to minister, and to give his life a ransom for many." **MARK 10:43–45**

The world defines greatness by power, position, privilege, and prestige. Greatness is the power to receive honor, the position of self-advancement, the privilege to be served, and the prestige of personal glory. Christ, however, gives us a radically different definition of greatness—it is the power to give honor, the position of self-abasement, the privilege to serve, and the prestige of God's glory.

Christ not only defined greatness, but he also demonstrated it. He showed us that humility is the first step to greatness. In Matthew 23:12 He said: "And whosoever shall exalt himself shall be abased; and he that shall humble himself shall be exalted."

The Creator of the universe condescended to become one of His own creation. Christ came as a servant to minister to men. Philippians 2:7 tells us that He "...made himself of no reputation, and took upon him the form of a servant...." He came not to seek His own good, but the good of others, not His glory but the glory of His Father. While He was on Earth, He mingled with the outcasts, the lowly, and the poor, and served them. He washed the feet of His disciples, healed the sick, comforted the hurting, and fed the hungry crowd.

Ultimately, Christ came to give His life a ransom for us. His ultimate goal was to redeem mankind; therefore, He humbled Himself even to death, allowing those

He came to serve to nail Him to the cross. His greatness was displayed from the beginning in His birth to the very end in His death.

God calls us to greatness—the greatness of humility and servanthood. Desire to be great today; desire to be His servant.

REFLECT

What did God say to me as I read today's Scripture and devotion?

RESPOND

How does this apply to my life? What actions can I take because of what I've learned?

PRAY

"Lord, thank You for showing me what true greatness is. Mold my life after Your model of servanthood. Help me not to seek self, but to serve others. Please help me to define greatness by Your standards rather than this world's. Clothe me in humility that I may be an effective servant for You. Amen."

ABOUT THE AUTHOR

Dr. Paul Chappell is the senior pastor of Lancaster Baptist Church and the president of West Coast Baptist College in Lancaster, California. He is a powerful communicator of God's Word and a passionate servant to God's people. He has been married to his wife, Terrie, since 1980, and they have four married children who are all serving in Christian ministry. He enjoys spending time with his family and serving the Lord shoulder to shoulder with a wonderful church family.

Dr. Chappell's preaching is heard on Daily in the Word, a radio program that is broadcast across America. You can find a station listing at paulchappell.com/radio.

You can also connect with Dr. Chappell here:

Blog: paulchappell.com
Twitter: twitter.com/paulchappell
Facebook: facebook.com/pastor.paul.chappell

BOOKS YOU'LL LOVE FROM PAUL CHAPPELL...

Trust and Obey

365 Devotions to Encourage Your Walk of Faith

Paul Chappell's *Trust and Obey* devotional will encourage your spiritual growth. The readings conclude with a solid takeaway principle which you can apply to your life immediately. You'll be challenged and encouraged to follow Jesus more closely and to walk with Him in practical ways throughout each day.

Are We There Yet?

Marriage—The Perfect Journey
for Imperfect Couples

This book is for every couple at any stage of the marriage journey. It will help reveal a God-given perspective that can change and strengthen your marriage. A companion guide is sold separately.

Making Home Work in a Broken Society

Bible Principles for Raising Children
and Building Families

God has entrusted you, as a parent, to care for and raise your children for Him—but it's not easy. Discover what it means to invest in your children and how you can bring them up in the nurture and admonition of the Lord.

STRIVINGTOGETHER.COM

ALSO AVAILABLE AS EBOOKS